Harriette Merrick Hodge Plunkett

Josiah Gilbert Holland

Harriette Merrick Hodge Plunkett

Josiah Gilbert Holland

ISBN/EAN: 9783743321687

Manufactured in Europe, USA, Canada, Australia, Japa

Cover: Foto ©ninafisch / pixelio.de

Manufactured and distributed by brebook publishing software (www.brebook.com)

Harriette Merrick Hodge Plunkett

Josiah Gilbert Holland

Josiah Gilbert Holland

BY

MRS. H. M. PLUNKETT

WITH PORTRAITS AND ILLUSTRATIONS

NEW YORK
CHARLES SCRIBNER'S SONS
1894

COPYRIGHT, 1894, BY
CHARLES SCRIBNER'S SONS

TROW DIRECTORY
PRINTING AND BOOKBINDING COMPANY
NEW YORK

To the

WIFE

WHO SO FAITHFULLY WALKED AT DR. HOLLAND'S SIDE

THIS BOOK IS AFFECTIONATELY DEDICATED

BY

HER FRIEND OF MANY YEARS

H. M. P.

PREFATORY NOTE

J. G. HOLLAND has been dead thirteen years, and hitherto no formal record of his life has been put forth.

To perpetuate the memory of a man whose name was, for many years, a household word, this book has been undertaken. So much of it is taken from his own works, that, in a measure, it is an autobiographical chronicle, and so much of the remainder is made up of the judgment of others concerning him and his works, that the part taken by the person whose name appears on the title-page, resembles that of the cement in a mosaic, which unites and retains in position materials already prepared.

But as it has grown under her hand, it has seemed, more and more, a work eminently worthy of being done.

H. M. P.

PITTSFIELD, MASS., February, 1894.

CONTENTS

CHAPTER I.

PAGES

Boyhood and Early Home—Ancestry—Inherited Traits—His Father and Mother—Life at Northampton—School-days and Factory-work—Early Evidence of Literary Bent, ... 1–12

CHAPTER II.

First Literary Production—Study at the High School—Delicate Health—Becomes a Writing master—Studies Medicine — Abandons Medicine for Journalism, ... 13–23

CHAPTER III.

Marriage to Miss Elizabeth Chapin—Partnership with Dr. Charles Robinson — Abandons Medicine — A Teacher in Richmond—Superintendent of Schools in Vicksburg—Begins his Newspaper Career—The "Springfield Republican"—The History of Western Massachusetts, ... 24–35

CHAPTER IV.

The Apostle to the New Englanders takes up his Mission—The "Timothy Titcomb" Letters—Publishes his First Book—"Gold Foil," 36–43

CONTENTS

CHAPTER V.

His First Novel, and the Beginning of his Lecturing Career — "Bittersweet," "Miss Gilbert's Career," and the Civil War—Eulogy on Lincoln, . . . 44-56

CHAPTER VI.

Undertakes the "Life of Lincoln" — Complete Harmony with his Subject—View of Lincoln's Essential Traits — His Religious Side and Deep Melancholy,. 57-67

CHAPTER VII.

Becomes the Possessor of "Brightwood"—A Pioneer in Domestic Sanitation—Publication of "Kathrina"— Invited to Edit *Hours at Home*—European Sojourn — Founding of *Scribner's Monthly*—Death of Mr. Scribner—Illustrations of the Magazine—Pride in his Lay Pulpit, ... 68-84

CHAPTER VIII.

Robert Collyer on the Success of *Scribner's Monthly*, and the quality of "Topics of the Time"—First Symptoms of Heart Disease—Character of his Editorial Contributions — Lessons from the Deaths of Fisk and Tweed—The Revised Version of the Bible—Dogmatic Theology, ... 85-98

CHAPTER IX.

The Elements of Dr. Holland's Power—His Religious Experience—Account of Judge Underhill—Spiritual Experience at Richmond—Church Work at Springfield,. 99-111

CONTENTS

CHAPTER X.

PAGES

Church Connections—Dr. Gladden's Memorial Sermon—Influence of Dr. Drummond — Formation of the Memorial Church — Association with the "Brick Church"—Teaching Sunday School in Paris—Conversation with Mr. De Vries — "Arthur Bonnicastle," 112–127

CHAPTER XI.

Literary Success a Plant of Slow Growth — "Bitter-Sweet" published when he was Forty—Criticisms of It—James Russell Lowell's review in *The Atlantic Monthly*—"Thanksgiving Day"—Observations on the Bible, ... 128–145

CHAPTER XII.

Publication of "Kathrina"—Dr. Holland's Doctrine of Art a Ministry—Sudden Death in October, 1881—Poetical Tributes of E. C. Stedman and Dr. Gladden, ... 146–158

CHAPTER XIII.

Memorial Services—In Springfield, New York, Alexandria Bay, and Belchertown — Eulogies of Edward Eggleston, George S. Merriam, and Others — Dr. Bevan's Sermon — Discourse of Rev. P. W. Lyman, ... 159–182

CHAPTER XIV.

Dr. Holland's Will — Tribute of his Associates in the Magazine Editorship — The Secular Press on his Power and its Sources — Tribute of the Religious Papers—His Family, Grave, and Monument, . 183–208

LIST OF ILLUSTRATIONS

PORTRAIT OF J. G. HOLLAND (*from a photograph by Sarony*), ... *Frontispiece*

                                              FACING PAGE

BIRTHPLACE OF DR. HOLLAND, BELCHERTOWN, MASS.   1

PORTRAIT OF MRS. HOLLAND, ... 24

J. G. HOLLAND—1860,   44

THE BUFF COTTAGE, .   . . 70

BRIGHTWOOD, ...   88

BONNIE CASTLE, ... 122

DR. HOLLAND'S GRAVE, ... 208

The Birthplace of Dr. Holland
Belchertown, Mass.

JOSIAH GILBERT HOLLAND

CHAPTER I.

Boyhood and Early Home—Ancestry—Inherited Traits—His Father and Mother—Life at Northampton—School-days and Factory-work—Early Evidence of Literary Bent.

An English statesman, on being asked the best way in which to produce a brilliant man, replied, "Give him parts and poverty." Nature gave Josiah Gilbert Holland parts, and circumstances supplied a degree of poverty that spurred him to the utmost use and improvement of his powers; and yet he was eminently well-born, for his industrious and upright parents could trace their origin back to the very beginning of New England through a succession of the typically diligent and pious men and women who gave the region its distinctive character.

John and Judith Holland were members of the church that was formed in Plymouth, England, and emigrated with their pastor to Dorchester, Mass.; and whatever thread of Dr. Holland's ancestry we trace to its beginnings, brings us to one of those God-fearing Puritans who settled about the "Bay."

His mother was born in Hebron, Conn., but grew up to womanhood in the Gilbert homestead in Belchertown, Mass., and in that town his father came to man's estate, and the twain were married November 5, 1810. In 1812 the town passed through a remarkable revival of religion, and among the one hundred and seven converts who united with the church in consequence, were Mr. Harrison Holland and his wife, Anna Gilbert. The husband was known ever afterward as a modest, thoroughly earnest Christian, and the impression made by what the old-fashioned New England ministers called his "walk and conversation" is described by his son in the poem of "Daniel Gray," printed in the *Atlantic Monthly* in 1859. It is as follows:

    If I shall ever win the home in heaven
  For whose sweet rest I humbly hope and pray,
      In the great company of the forgiven
  I shall be sure to find old Daniel Gray.

    .   .   .   .

    Old Daniel Gray was not a man who lifted
      On ready words his freight of gratitude,
    And was not called upon among the gifted,
      In the prayer-meetings of his neighborhood.

    .   .   .   .

He had a hearty hatred of oppression,
    And righteous words for sin of every kind ;
Alas, that the transgressor and transgression
    Were linked so closely in his honest mind !

Yet that sweet tale of gift without repentance
    Told of the Master, touched him to the core,
And tearless he could never read the sentence :
    "Neither do I condemn thee : sin no more."
    .   .   .   .

A practical old man, and yet a dreamer,
    He thought that in some strange, unlooked-for way
His mighty Friend in heaven, the great Redeemer,
    Would honor him with wealth some golden day.

This dream he carried in a hopeful spirit
    Until in death his patient eye grew dim,
And his Redeemer called him to inherit
    The heaven of wealth long garnered up for him.

The wife and mother would certainly be classed among persons then described as "devoted," and it was the deeply religious character of these parents that so stamped itself on the son, that he inevitably viewed men and events first and chiefly from the moral standpoint. He resembled his mother in features and physique, but derived his mental characteristics from his father—with a difference.

His father owned and ran a carding-machine, and, sixty years ago, when all the woollen yarns, and most of the flannel and blankets, and much of the

cloth worn by men were of domestic manufacture—
"homespun"—his was an important industry; but
a single carding-machine, though owned by its operator, was but an inadequate instrument with which
to win bread for a wife and six children, even in the
most strenuous hands; and in the transition to
"factories" that took place between 1820 and 1840,
it was quite displaced and superseded. Moreover,
its owner was essentially a dreamer. He was always
inventing ingenious trifles, and sometimes made
verses, and held the fatuously sanguine view that
some other place and some distant morrow held a
boon and blessing denied to the here and now.

> "For while he wrought with strenuous will
>   The work his hands had found to do,
> He heard the fitful music still
>   Of winds that out of dream-land blew;
> The din about him could not drown
>   What the strange voices whispered round."

Among his other inventions, worked out after his
older sons had gone into a silk-mill, was a reel for
holding the silk when unwound from the cocoon.
The power of the almost infinitesimal "royalty" on
patented articles to build up colossal fortunes had
not then been demonstrated, and Mr. Holland's
honorable and confiding spirit could not imagine the
unprincipled meanness that would deliberately rob

a man of the fruits of his brain; and, besides, very likely he could not command the small but indispensable sum of ready money needed to obtain a patent. So others reaped where he had sown; but the invention itself was so complete and opportune that the raw silk comes from China to-day wound on the machine that he invented.

Following that *ignis fatuus*, through which he was always "to be blessed," he removed from Belchertown to Heath, back again, thence to Granby, and from there to South Hadley; but finally, and where the household "made a stand," to Northampton. His old business had long before this vanished wholly, so that when living in Granby, when Josiah was about fifteen years old, his visible means of support had dwindled to casual day's-work for farmers, and the family resources were eked out by the braiding of palm-leaf hats by the daughters. His poverty touched the lowest point at this period. He said to an old friend afterward: "My poverty turned when I left South Hadley. I had not a pound of meat nor a handful of flour left, and I didn't know where the next meal was to come from." During the short time lived in that town, the family had occupied no fewer than three different houses, and afterward, in alluding to the removal to Northampton, Dr. Holland said "the Holland family concluded not to move any more," accompanying the remark with a look which clearly conveyed the notion that the decision was largely his own; and there is no doubt that, though only seventeen years of age, he had passed the Rubicon that separates boyhood from manhood, and become the leading spirit that was to dominate the plans and fortunes not only of himself, but of the family as well.

Some of the pictures in "Miss Gilbert's Career" and "Arthur Bonnicastle" are believed to have been drawn from personal experiences of their author. But though the home was poor, it was the abode of affection, and above all of that peace that passeth understanding; for the mother, as well as the father, possessed a rarely beautiful and serene character. Anna Gilbert Holland was a typical New England wife and mother, whose ideals of woman's sphere and wifely duty had been formed from her earliest childhood on the models set forth in the Scriptures; and moreover, from the time when she had been "converted" there had been added that lofty spirit of self-abnegation and submission to the Divine Will, that was designated "devoted." From the time when her reception into the visible church announced to the world that her face was set toward the heavenly city, her soul dwelt in the atmosphere of the eternal and the invisible—she looked on the life that now is as merely the staging that was to serve in building up a character that should eventually win the Master's "well done;" and as the days—which in a family where there were six or seven children, were inevitably full of care—glided by she literally felt that,

> "She nightly pitched her moving tent
> A day's march nearer home."

It is easy for the flippant critic of the Puritans to sneer at their strictness and to deplore what the said critic regards as their bare and cheerless lives; but the sun never looked down upon sweeter, purer, or happier homes than theirs, where the day began with a prayer for strength to meet its vicissitudes, and closed with a grateful recognition of its mercies. Mrs. Holland was full of that womanly courage and patience that met the inevitable difficulties of life cheerfully. The "heart of her husband safely trusted in her," and she was the staff on which he leaned when his pecuniary troubles were at their darkest; and it was always a matter of thankfulness with Dr. Holland that she outlived his father, who was very dependent on her serene Christian courage. At about the time when Dr. Holland attained his majority, a deep shadow fell upon her life in the death, in the compass of fifteen months, of her three daughters—two of consumption and one of measles. She never recovered from the blow, and nothing in her son's life is more beautiful than the tender forethought and devotion through which he strove to make her forget her sorrow.

Sixty years ago the chasm that separates the rich from the poor was by no means as wide as it is to-day, and New England possessed an order of aristocracy whose claims are hinted at in Cowper's

> "But higher far my proud pretensions rise,
> The son of parents passed into the skies,"

and a family whose united heads belonged to the church, and whose lives matched their professions, belonged to that high order of respectability, not to say nobility. Dr. Holland personally belonged to that class of persons "whose souls by nature sit on thrones," no matter by what degree of poverty or of misfortune obscured. There was not a particle of arrogance in him, but it never occurred to him that he was not the peer in respectability of any man, and in one of his books, where a discussion is going on as to the relative shades of blueness in the blood of certain families, he goes right to the heart of the matter by making the speaker say, "God makes new Adams every day." Certainly He makes some men with such an irrepressible bent toward this or that line of work, that they cannot escape this destiny of their faculties. J. G. Holland was one of these, although it took till he was thirty years old for him to make sure of his work and place in the world—to fulfil his mission and deliver his message—with what indefatigable faithfulness wrought out and delivered, let his life-story tell; for it may as well be said, first as last, that no matter what literary form—poem, story, essay—his writings took, he was essentially a preacher, and ever and always an expounder of those things that make for righteousness. If ever his sad-hearted mother had a dream for him, it was that he might be a minister; and when she once expressed a regret that her wish had not been granted, he pointed out the larger sphere of influence given him in the newspaper, though he hardly thought she was convinced.

Of course, it was the "visionary" dreaming father who was quick to discern the subtle something that differentiated this boy, and showed him to be out of the common, and he cherished every line of his verses, no matter how boyish or juvenile. When so young as to sleep in a trundle-bed beside his parents, he called out: "Oh, Father, I've made a verse!" and repeated,

> "I like a little pigeon,
>   I think it is very good meat,
> But in the colder region
>   They have no pigeon to eat."

It merely shows the tendency of his thoughts to clothe themselves in ordered words, for, in those days were no children's books, or magazines, or journals full of every sort of stimulus to precocious literary efforts ; but the careful writing out and preservation of it by the father shows to what quarter the son would look for an approving, encouraging smile, when, later, his powers should begin to unfold.

Wherever the family had lived the boys had attended the public schools, picking up whatever stray pennies they could earn by driving the cows to pasture, or " doing chores ;" but when the family were in South Hadley, Josiah went regularly to work in a factory, boarding in the common boarding-house. The overseer of the room in which he worked said he was "dreamy" and abstracted, and frequently reproved him for letting his threads break, or for being too slow in mending them. On one occasion, having been specially offensive in his manner, the boy drew himself up to his full height, and with defiant eyes said, "I'll give you to understand, if I live many years, I was born for something other than to tend a spinning-jenny!" Poverty had indeed knotted a whip of scorpions to scourge him to the utmost use of his faculties, that he might escape from an utterly distasteful life. Mrs. Stowe says that the only dissipation New England girls of those far-away times knew, was to go to each other's houses to sleep, and then lie awake all night and talk; and certainly it was a great relief and delight for at least two boys, in the secluded part of South Hadley, where a friend of Josiah's then lived. Though he was not yet seventeen, many of the grave subjects afterward discussed in the letters to various persons by Timothy Titcomb, were talked or rather "lectured" over in the nights of these days, of which M. S. Mills Cook, of Granby, still retains a vivid memory. Books were a rarity in the Holland home —not even a county paper was taken—and Josiah's only resource to satisfy the intellectual craving that he felt, was to borrow from the severely "orthodox" minister—Parson Moody—his standard works in divinity by Emmons, Griffin, Hopkins, and Edwards, all of which were read through, and as one after another was completed and returned, the good man predicted that "that boy would make his mark in the world."

Let no one imagine that he was deficient in virile and positive qualities, because he eschewed profanity and every form of coarseness. At school he was ready for the boyish "tussle" that would show "who was who," and won the championship so squarely from "the other big boy" as to be thenceforth the legitimate object of the hero-worship of the little fellows. His irrepressible propensity for writing exercised itself on all possible topics and occasions; his "compositions" generally were in verse, and one quite ambitious "Address to the Comet," sent his teachers off into predictions of future fame; while his love for, and facility in acquiring, words easily made him the victor in all the spelling matches.

CHAPTER II.

First Literary Production—Study at the High School—Delicate Health—Becomes a Writing master—Studies Medicine—Abandons Medicine for Journalism.

BEFORE the Holland family reached its last and fortunate home in Northampton, the boy had formed the resolution "to be an educated gentleman"— these are his own words—a resolve that he kept constantly in mind, though he passed through many dark and discouraging hours. Northampton had a superior High School, and that he determined to attend; but to relieve the household of expense on his account, he became an inmate of Judge Dewey's family, rendering those multifarious services comprehended in the phrase "doing chores for his board." It was while living here that he first saw a product of his pen in print—a poem founded on the fact that a little son of Judge Dewey had planted a tree in his father's grounds which continued to live after the boy had died, and was cherished as a precious memento by the parents. The incident supplied a substratum for four verses, which were sent to the *Youth's Companion*, then a twelve by fourteen sheet, but the only publication of its class in all New England, if not in the country. Long after this, when Dr. Holland's books were read by the hundred thousands, a literary club in Ohio, which had taken up his life and writings for discussion, asked him to oblige them by relating some incident in his life that had never been in print. He complied by saying, "The first article of mine that ever saw the light was a little poem of four stanzas, entitled, 'James's Tree.' It was published in the *Youth's Companion*, a publication still prosperous. I was then seventeen years old, and that was forty-four years ago. I took the printed copy containing it from the Post-office, peeped within, and then walked home on air. I shall probably never be so absorbingly happy as I was then. Earth has nothing like it—earth never had anything like it—for me. I have seen my work in type since then, till I have tired of the sight of it, but I can never forget the great joy of that occasion. The poem was signed 'J. G. H., Aug. 18, 1837.'"

While he was pursuing his high-school course a shadow rested on his life and prospects, in the shape of delicate health, but he worked on resolved to do till he did die, at all events. The causes were partly mental and partly physical. The transition from a life of activity to the sedentary one of the student, was what the doctors said was the matter, and the stirrings of the ambition that was to carry him through long years of struggle were making themselves felt. Moreover, a false idea permeated the whole community, that a man who was "merely studying" did not need much to eat. The "pale intellectual" slave of the midnight lamp was the ideal of the scholar, and much of the fearful dyspepsia that drove Sylvester Graham to invent his kind of flour and bread, in this same Northampton, was the fruit of this notion. The beef-and-mutton-eating athlete had not appeared in our colleges. The great majority of students did not eat enough.

Years afterward, when success had surrounded him with every luxury, a friend who knew what constitutional weaknesses and fastidious hesitancies have to be overcome before a man can study medicine to any purpose, said to him, "It always amuses me to think of your having ever undertaken to be a doctor, it is so incongruous; with your instinctive shrinkiug from the sight of pain and deformity, the whole business must have been distasteful to you." "It was," said he, "but you forget what a different world we live in to-day; now there are a hundred avenues opened where there was one then, and I was determined to be an educated gentleman, and for that you had to take one of three paths: I could be a minister, but that required a college course which my poverty utterly forbade. I should have been middle-aged before I could possibly have achieved it. I felt no drawing toward the law, the more I knew of it the less I liked it ; but medicine—that could be attained with a far less outlay of money and of time, and the successful physician presented a very attractive figure among the magnates of a New England town."

His health had mended with his growth, and the delicate adolescent had become a fairly strong man. The comparatively small sum that would be required for a medical education, must be in some way earned, so he acquired a hand-writing singularly delicate, clear, uniform, and attractive ; page after page would not show the trace of a nervous tremor, and an old foreman in the *Springfield Republican* printing-office testified, that even under the insatiate, all-devouring demand of a daily newspaper for "copy," it still remained "as plain as print." At that date—1838—the metallic pen had not been invented, and the art of making pens from the native goose-quill was an accomplishment to be learned by everybody with any pretensions to education ; so young Holland started out as a writing-master, and instructed large classes in Northampton and the adjacent towns, even going over the border into Vermont. He had the good fortune to inspire great enthusiasm in all his classes, putting all the zeal and force there was in him into the work of the hour, and as he passed from place to place, boarding often by way of compensation for lessons in some farmer's family, he was learning the traits and needs, the trials and difficulties, of those "common people," who so eagerly drank in instruction and help from his writings, after he had finally found his place and work in life.

But, though struggling against poverty, his life was far from being a joyless grind. His sensitive musical ear, and his fine tenor voice, always made him welcome in the local singing schools, and his leisure moments were quite sure to fill themselves with the writing of verses; these he often contributed to the *Hampshire Gazette*. Some of them are still extant, and though tender and refined, they are evidently the productions of an unlearned, untravelled, homebred country boy.

When twenty-one, he at last began to realize his dream of a professional education, by commencing the study of medicine in the office of Drs. Barrett and Thompson, where he applied himself with unremitting industry to the acquisition of the necessary knowledge, and, after he had attained eminence in another field, a drawing of the entire human arterial system that he had made on the wall of the office from memory, was pointed out as a proof of his ability.

To obtain the degree of M.D. required, at that time, that a man should read medicine under some reputable "preceptor" two years, but that time must include two terms of lectures of three months each, in some regularly authorized medical school. The Berkshire Medical College in Pittsfield, under the energetic presidency of Dr. H. H. Childs, was a justly famous school, and Dr. Holland took his degree from it, November 3, 1843.

The annual irruption of the students and professors—many of them eminent instructors in other schools—was of course a very enlivening event in a quiet inland town of five thousand people. A Young Ladies' School, whose principal was a progressive man, and whose quick ear had caught the first sounds of the demand for the "higher education of women," had arranged that the most advanced pupils should attend the chemical lectures then being given in the college by Professor Dewey. Of course, the girls were full of excitement at the prospect, and betrayed their consciousness in the matter by all agreeing to wear thick veils made of a very obscuring tissue called "barège," which were to be kept over the features during the lectures, and there was a general agreement to "cut" the students wherever found.

The *Pittsfield Sun* soon printed
"*Stanzas to Rather Distant Friends*,"
beginning thus:

> "Stay, gentle maidens—why so shy?
> I'm sure you need not fear us;
> Why draw the veil, avert the eye,
> Whenever you come near us?

> Why should you deem it so unwise,
> Improper, and imprudent,
> To turn a pair of handsome eyes
> Upon a handsome student?"

The verses were signed, "*Nothing but a Student*," the quotation marks showing them to be the echo of a contemptuous expression. Naturally, curiosity was on tiptoe to discover the author, but the incognito was not penetrated for a long time. At that age of the world the American chaperone had not made her appearance, certainly not in the rural regions, yet none but students carefully introduced could gain admission to the aristocratic households of the place; but judging from the large number of medical men who obtained their mates in the town, we conclude that many students provided themselves with unimpeachable credentials. The line of exclusiveness piqued a proud-spirited young fellow, in whose hitherto rustic surroundings he had been accustomed to say to himself, no matter whom he met, "I'm as good as you are, and if I know myself, possibly better." The first set of verses called out a reply from some unknown hand, and he rejoined in a dozen verses, in which he rudely applied the *argumentum ad feminam*, thus:

> "We cannot '*cut*' a dash, perhaps,
> As some rich loafers do,

> But does that prove we studious chaps
> Should all be *cut* by you?
> No doubt you think us all unfit
> To act the tender part;
> You're wrong, we all know how to treat
> *Affections* of the *heart.*"

In the thesis then required from a student before he could be graduated, he took for his theme the comparatively unmedical theme, "The Theory of Sensation;" and, in his neat and delicate chirography, it still exists among the archives of the now defunct Berkshire Medical College. Of course he was obliged to practise the greatest economy, and he took board with such an exceedingly thrifty housewife, that one of his principal associations with the time was that of being always hungry, and of having imbibed a large amount of the weakest coffee ever distilled.

The coveted diploma once secured he returned to Northampton, and here he found the social recognition that he craved, and during the winter, at a party given by Editor Hawley, of the *Gazette*, he first saw the lady who afterward became his wife; and though not then introduced to her, she had made a lasting impression, as events finally proved. In some way he had acquired quite an acquaintance in Springfield, which was then just beginning to feel the impulse imparted by its first railroad, travel on the line which extends from Boston to Albany had been opened in 1842. In the spring of 1844 he went there to look over the ground, with a view to establishing himself in practice, and accidentally met on State Street Dr. Charles Bailey, a classmate, who had come thither from the eastern part of the State on a similar errand, and then and there they decided upon and fixed the terms of a partnership. Dr. Bailey could command a little money, and it was agreed that Dr. Holland's "acquaintance" should be considered equivalent to the other's money, and they rented an office in Main Street. It is a hard task for an enthusiastic devotee of the science to build up a medical practice, and certainly the thoughts of one of these partners were not absorbed by his business, as one incident will show. The teacher of a young ladies' boarding-school had seen Dr. Holland, been favorably impressed, and decided to employ him. Two of her pupils were attacked with scarlatina, and she sent for him. But what did he do with the grand opening? The call came when he was at work on a poem that he called "The Fays of the Fountain," and he said, "You go, Bailey; make some excuse; tell 'em I can't come." The want of professional enthusiasm that could coolly miss such an opportunity, carried its doom within itself, and at the end of two and a half years the partnership was dissolved by mutual consent.

Still, during the time he had answered one urgent call that had an important consequence in his afterlife. An epidemic of malignant erysipelas broke out in the town of Norwich. Dr. Brooks, a classmate of Dr. Holland, had settled there, and being himself attacked, in the emergency sent to him to come to the rescue of the smitten town. Antiseptic measures had not been heard of then, and, as this outbreak had shown itself to be very " catching," it was thought a great risk for Dr. Holland to go ; but he listened to the call of humanity as well as professional duty, and remained till the trouble was extirpated. He had made a steadfast friend of Dr. Brooks, who was able to lend him assistance at an important crisis in his own career, and remained ever a sincerely attached admirer and friend.

Before his medical partnership had ended, his irrepressible bent toward literary work had shown itself in the publication of *The Bay State Weekly Courier*, whose brief history is given in Dr. Holland's own words in his " History of Western Massachusetts : " " On the 1st of January, 1847, a literary newspaper was commenced by J. G. Holland, a physician, as a refuge from uncongenial pills, and a still more uncongenial lack of opportunity for dispensing them. At the end of about three months he relinquished the proprietorship of the paper to Horace S. Taylor, its printer, he still remaining its editor. At the end of about six months the paper was discontinued for lack of support. The publication was nominally simultaneous in Springfield and Cabotville. The list was sold to the *Republican*."

CHAPTER III.

Marriage to Miss Elizabeth Chapin—Partnership with Dr. Charles Robinson—Abandons Medicine—A Teacher in Richmond—Superintendent of Schools in Vicksburg—Begins his Newspaper Career—The "Springfield Republican"—The History of Western Massachusetts.

But in 1845 Dr. Holland had taken another step that had a controlling and beneficent influence on all his future life, by doing what the Rev. Robert Collyer calls "the best day's work that a man ever does for himself—that in which he takes a wife and establishes a home "—by marrying Miss Elizabeth Chapin, of Springfield, and any account of his remarkable career which leaves her out is most partial and incomplete. Her strong practical judgment was an offset to his more imaginative temperament, and, though making no literary pretensions herself, she was a remarkably sympathetic and correct judge of what it is that appeals to, and influences, and is valued by that great company of "the plain people," as Abraham Lincoln called them, whom eventually her husband was to address to such purpose. But it was the stern Puritan industry and

Mrs. Holland

frugality of the woman, who at all hazards—no matter what the sacrifice—would keep the outgo within the income, that created the serene atmosphere of peace and hope about him, into which no spectre of debt and consequent uneasiness could intrude to disturb the fruitful current of his thought. A typical womanly woman, she never for one moment remitted her wifely pride in the gentlemanly appearance of her eminently handsome husband. When a new overcoat was essential to his comfort and his looks, the cloth was bought by her, the garment cut by a stylish tailor, but the sewing was done at home by a peripatetic tailoress, and an excellent effect achieved at less than half the cost that most men would have paid. Their life-story holds a moral for these days of late marriages, in which the "sweet" home, whose most precious perfume is distilled from the mutual sacrifices of both husband and wife, is far rarer than it used to be. A miniature of Mrs. Holland made at this time, shows her with a fair complexion, a rosy bloom, a pair of remarkably frank and fearless bluish-gray eyes, and a wealth of soft brown hair. She was of medium height, but looked fairly petite beside the tall and stalwart figure of her husband. His dark-olive complexion and black eyes and hair gave him a Spanish look, but when illuminated in talking or in lecturing, his face had a remarkable brilliancy of expression, and the two presented that happy contrast which some philosophers deem essential to perfect mutual admiration in husband and wife.

After his first partnership had come to nought, he formed another with Dr. Charles Robinson—a Belchertown boy and a Pittsfield graduate, who afterward went to Kansas and was its governor, when in fact it was "bleeding Kansas," and who still survives in an honored old age. They undertook to establish a hospital for women, a desperate experiment—quite in advance of the time—for the day of the specialist and the sanitarium was only beginning to dawn. Six months served to complete this experiment, and convince Dr. Holland that the tree of medicine bore no fruit for his plucking. He was gaining a world of experience and discipline, but of cash—nil. At that date, the South drew largely on the North for its schoolmasters, and he accepted a position as teacher in a private school in Richmond, Va., and very soon afterward—through the good offices of a friend—he was elected to the superintendency of the Public Schools of Vicksburg, Miss., and Mrs. Holland, who had not gone with him to Richmond, accompanied him to the more distant field. A state of chaos best describes the condition of the schools there at that time. He at once set about applying the ideas he had acquired in Massachusetts, whose educational system at that time rejoiced in the inspiration of Horace Mann. He graded the schools, and in spite of many prognostications to the contrary, made a brilliant success by doing with his might the work his hand found to do. Mrs. Holland had married him for "richer or poorer," and at this juncture it was decidedly poorer, and she taught the primary department, earning $10 per week—just enough to pay their board. The year 1848 was long remembered as a golden year in the history of the Vicksburg schools. In the vacation he accepted an invitation to visit on one of the largest plantations in Louisiana, and of course the irrepressible pen had to come into play. He wrote "Sketches of Plantation Life" and sent them to the *Springfield Republican*, and undoubtedly they led up to his finally reaching his right place in life. At the same time he sent poems to the *Home Journal* and the *Knickerbocker Magazine*.

When he had been in Vicksburg a year and three months, letters came saying that Mrs. Holland's widowed mother was probably near death, and her own health was such as made it expedient that the hard journey, much of it in stage-coach and over the Allegheny Mountains, should not be delayed. The superintendency was resigned, and they reached Springfield two weeks before Mrs. Chapin's death. A son was born to them in the following August.

The story has often been told that the second "Editor Bowles," known the world over as "Sam Bowles," stood in the office door as Dr. Holland drove up the street, and seeing him, said "That is the man I want," while the doctor, pointing to the building, said "That is the place I want." And as they thus thought it eventually was, for the assistant editor, Samuel H. Davis, of Westfield, had been buried shortly before, and the "place" and the "man" were not long in finding each other, and in two weeks' time Dr. Holland was made assistant editor. At last the man had found his niche, and all unconsciously to himself, the lay preacher had taken possession of his pulpit.

He was now thirty, and it had taken nine years of changes and experiments for him to find, as Mr. Gladden happily says, "the tool that he had been looking for, with which to carve out fame and fortune; and behold, it was a pen!" His salary for the first year was $40 per month—$480; the second year $700, and during the third he was able to buy a quarter interest in the paper for $3,500, the Dr. Brooks, whose practice in Norwich Dr. Holland had cared for during the erysipelas epidemic, making him a small loan, which was not only an offering of gratitude, but was the proof of an abiding friendship.

Mr. Bowles was only twenty-five at this time,

but all the world knows what a marvel of journalism he produced in a quiet inland town, creating a paper that had a national reputation. One of the great elements of its success was his unerring sagacity in the choice of helpers. If he had an unequalled "nose for news," he also had a wonderful eye for men, as well as the quick instinctive feeling of what the public wants, and will pay for, and will read. His discriminating glance detected among the graduates emerging from our New England colleges each year, men who now fill high positions in the newspaper world, men who could really assist him; and a long catalogue of these might be made, who took part of their schooling in the *Republican* office. Mr. Clarke W. Bryan was then editor of the *Berkshire Courier*, at Great Barrington, and he displayed so great executive ability in the collection of election returns for the paper, that it was the most natural thing in the world for him to be invited to come in; the more, as in 1853 Mr. Bowles's eyesight became seriously affected, and in this year a further division of labor and refinement of organization placed the printing and publication department under his complete supervision. Everybody at once perceived that a remarkable trio of young men, with life and hope and their careers before them, had planted themselves in the heart of New England, and the evolution of the newspaper in their hands, to a position of commanding influence—the story of which was told in its issue of December 8, 1888, forms a unique recital in the annals of country journalism. Dr. Holland, sitting in the editorial room—a very modest apartment—pen in hand, ready to write up notices of any size and style, from the establishment of a new peanut stand to the building of a Union railway station, or a review of the most ambitious book of the day, as well as to pronounce rhadamanthine judgments on the productions of spring poets and "constant readers;" Mr. Bowles, with one hand on the public pulse, detecting the slightest changes in the currents of thought and feeling, and in the other a telescope with which he swept the horizon, for the faintest glimpse of any new event—the tiniest glimmer of what would make even a line of Horace Greeley's "mighty interesting reading;" and the energetic Bryan, to see all printed, given out to newsboys or mailed on time, and that too every twenty-four hours, not to name the Weekly. Mr. Bowles once said: "It's the most wearing work on the face of the earth: you get the paper off, you catch one breath, and then it's, What's going in tomorrow?"

The vital need of every born writer is a public— that nebulous but always existent "party of the other part," that has been addressed in a thousand

CHARACTERISTICS AS EDITOR 31

timid prefaces as "the gentle reader." It is his natural environment, that reacts on him as the air does on the lungs; and Emerson never showed more perfectly his profound insight than when he doubted the vocation of some man whose literary gifts had been referred to him for judgment, saying, "I doubted his genius when I saw that he didn't care to publish."

In the interesting chronicle of the *Republican*, made up when it moved into its present building, it is said: "The advent of Dr. Holland as an editorial writer marks a distinct period in the importance given to social, humanitarian, and moral questions. His experience in a weekly paper devoted exclusively to literature did not dampen his literary ardor, and the experiment which was a failure in a business point of view was valuable to him, when he came to have both a proprietor's and an editor's interest in a daily paper. His style of composition had quality. It was both chaste and vigorous, and he readily acquired the art of popularizing a homily, by taking a text from the day's doings. The *Republican* began to commit itself upon social questions— the duties of employers and laborers, Sunday observance, and the like."

The idea that the newspaper must not only carry all of the latest news, but that it might bring, with great advantage to itself, far more to the home and fireside — entertainment, instruction, amusement — had then begun to be diffused in the land; such mammoth illustrated sheets as the *Brother Jonathan* had put in an appearance; and the city dailies were finding it worth their while to take pains in filling in odd spaces with really interesting matter. Of course, a man so sensitive to the spirit of the time as Mr. Bowles was not long in feeling this influence, nor slow in trying to meet the demand.

The circulation of the paper at this time was three thousand seven hundred for the daily edition, two-thirds of which was to out-of-town subscribers, and about four thousand for the weekly.

To make the paper interesting, Dr. Holland entered upon the work of studying and writing the history of Western Massachusetts, including the most complete account possible of the origin, progress, and condition of the one hundred towns that make up the four western counties of the State. Experienced historians thought it an undertaking of much audacity, for it was a work involving the discovering and deciphering no end of musty old documents, an immense correspondence, and a careful sifting of sometimes involved and conflicting accounts. Any error of statement was sure to be pounced upon by some "oldest inhabitant," but all this careful and accurate collating, comparing, and condensing was a splendid discipline for a natural verse-writer. It appeared serially in the *Weekly Republican*, but it was so much esteemed and prized, that he finally brought it out in two sizable volumes, that remain the leading authority on the period of which they treat, save for a few very minutely-written-out histories, like Judd's, of Hadley, or J. E. A. Smith's, of Pittsfield. The production of a serious and important book, forty years ago, was quite a different affair from what it is now, in the degree of personal distinction it conferred on its author. Dr. Holland was made a member of the Massachusetts Historical Society, but the work brought him a much more precious reward—it admitted him to the charmed circle of the "New England Brahmins," and he began to be recognized as that "educated gentleman" he had so earnestly determined to be when yet a school-boy. While accomplishing this, he formed the fixed habit of systematic application to his daily task; he waited for no moods, but worked right on, and as one who comprehended his achievements very truly says, "From the substantial success he achieved we may learn another lesson in life than any directly taught in his writings, to wit, the wonderful results of method and of industry in multiplying talent; in distinction from greater and higher gifts cultivated spasmodically. Talent and industry achieve in the end that which genius and idleness allied will never attain."

Before entering upon an account of the specific field where he achieved his greatest successes, viz., as an essential preacher of those things that make for righteousness in personal conduct—one element of his power in these days of excessive linguistic "education" should be noted—he spoke the speech of the common people, and when a plain man was reading one of his "Letters," or "Talks," or "Topics," all the "contrariness" of his soul was not stirred up by running across a Latin or French phrase or word, humiliating and disgusting him at his lack of "advantages." The short, forcible Saxon words of our tongue form the staple of his writing, he made no drafts on the sonorous polysyllabic Latinity of it, if he could avoid it. In his Memorial Address, Mr. George S. Merriam said, "He could think the thoughts and speak the speech of the common people. He represented that democratic quality in literature which our social conditions demand, and are only beginning to get. Take from your shelf at random a standard author other than a novelist, and read a page to the first man you chance to meet. Ten to one, he listens with a sort of uncomprehending look; the voice comes to him muffled, as of someone speaking in the next room, for most authors write out of a mental habit and equipment which is unfamiliar to the common people; they use a literary dialect—the dialect of a class, as much as is the dialect of science or theology. But take almost any book of Dr. Holland, and read it to any man or woman of common intelligence: the eye responds, they understand what he means; they agree or deny; they comprehend, they are moved, influenced. He was a man of the people, and the common people heard him gladly." However much the devotees of high literary "culture" may deplore what the critics are pleased to regard as his deficiencies, there are those whose hearts swell with gratitude that he was debarred by iron circumstance from acquiring that "learning," that so far forth would have unfitted him from ministering to the intellectual needs of the literal millions who read his productions, many of whom remember him for "some high impulse given when perhaps the will was faltering, some clear light shed when the path was dark." However facile the writer, he too comes under the unalterable law that "practice makes perfect;" no better proof is needed than to read his first set of letters to young people, and compare them with the compactness and finish, and rhythm of his latest "Topics of the Time" in *Scribner's Monthly*.

Dr. Bevan said of him, "He wielded a pen of consummate skill. I doubt whether better English has issued from the contemporary press of the last ten years than may be read in his 'Topics of the Time.'"

CHAPTER IV.

The Apostle to the New Englanders takes up his Mission— The "Timothy Titcomb" Letters—Publishes his First Book—"Gold Foil."

AFTER the completion of the historical series, Dr. Holland wrote the satirical letters of "Max Mannering to his Sister in the Country," and remaining incognito, aroused great interest in them. Mr. Bowles never showed his instinctive knowledge of what the public was hungering for more completely than when he suggested that a series of letters of moral advice would "take;" and certainly his editor, who whatever else was in a man, saw him first and principally as a moral agent whose watchword should be duty, and whose allegiance should be given to the One great invisible Leader, was the man to give the advice. To impart the desired air of venerability he chose the pseudonym of "Timothy Titcomb." They were written for the plain work-a-day people who plough, and sow, and reap, who spin and weave, and forge, and run our engines, and perform the myriad indispensable household tasks that are monotonous and commonplace, and often in such straitened circumstances, or accompanied by such trials and temptations, as to be well-nigh unbearable.

He addressed them on the commonest kinds of omissions and neglects, and as to phases of their lives; had he not seen them all, in the wanderings, and vicissitudes, and deprivations of his own? When a plain farmer's wife would hurry her bread into the oven, and seize her Saturday's paper and tear off the wrapper, saying, "I must see what 'Timothy Titcomb' says this week," before she washed her hands or looked at the marriages and deaths, we may believe that he spoke to a real want, and addressed an audience that was waiting to be taught.

It is impossible to reproduce the moral and mental attitude of our country at that time; we look back to it across the mighty chasm of a great civil war which revolutionized modes of thought and methods of living; which did much to dissipate the dreamy speculations of men who fancied themselves thinkers and leaders; it set up new standards in almost every department of life, but neither then nor now, was there ever a time when the true child of New England was indifferent to the questions What *is* Truth? and What ought *I* to do? Dr. Holland aimed to answer these questions for him. The knot of men in Boston who called themselves transcendentalists, and whose ideas were promulgated in the *Dial*, and whose attempts to improve the actual conditions of life took practical shape in Brook Farm, and who really loosened some of the foundation-stones of old outworn beliefs, were giving themselves to speculation on "The Whichness of the When, and the Whatness of the Why," when Dr. Holland was telling Yankee farmers that by a little more kindly forethought in "providing" they might save much suffering, and that hundreds of their wives died, annually, from green wood alone!

And while one of this sort was writing:

> "I rested by day with the formless;
> I talked with the stars of the night:
> I looked with the eyes of the viewless,
> And found in the darkness the light,"

he was telling cold and stern fathers and mothers how they were ruining the lives of their children by imposing their own iron wills on the young lives committed to their care, and never allowing them to be free from restraint.

At that time Mr. Emerson, after showing that the history of the world had crystallized about a few heroes, wrote this: "Broader and deeper we must write our annals, from an ethical reformation, from an influx of the ever new, ever sanative conscience —if we would trulier express our central and world-related nature, instead of this old chronology of selfishness and pride to which we have too long lent our eyes." Those men undoubtedly rendered literature, their country, and the world a service, but their lights shone so far up in the empyrean, that only the dwellers on the topmost eminences of learning and thought could really benefit by them; they did not send their rays down into the valleys, where dwell the multitudes of mankind.

The "Letters" were in three series—to young men, to young women, and to young married people —and were a great and immediate success, and their popularity soon began to tell in the subscription list of the paper. These were over and above the daily editorial work which was carried unremittingly forward. Nothing was more natural than that they should be gathered into a book and carried to a publisher. Two prominent firms "looked" at them and declined, and another declined them without looking. Armed with a letter of introduction from George Ripley, Dr. Holland went to the late Charles Scribner and begged the privilege of reading three of the letters. Mr. Scribner turned the key of his private office and bade the author proceed. At the end of the third letter he said, "I will take the book." A most sagacious decision, for at the time of Dr. Holland's death, in 1881, half a million of copies of this and his succeeding works had been sold, and their popularity continues practically unimpaired. Mr. Scribner recognized that there are different strata of readers, and that in the evolution of a man, he sometimes belongs to one and sometimes to another. This was the first of a series of fifteen books, that followed in fifteen years. The pyramid certainly is larger at its base than at its apex. A very discriminating editorial in the Boston *Traveller*, at the time of Dr. Holland's death, discloses the secret of his power. All agree that he was essentially a preacher, that he felt he had a message, and that he was bound to deliver it. The writer says: "It is difficult to estimate justly the real services Dr. Holland has rendered, not so much to literature, as to those whom Lincoln called the 'plain people.' In his 'Kathrina' the doctor elaborates a theory of how teachers stand between the great master minds and the people, to break the bread, to serve as interpreters." Nothing more accurately designates Dr. Holland's place in literature. "Books, like friends, have their special messages for us at special epochs of life, and missing these once, we must miss them forever. The best juvenile literature could not entrance us if we first met it after we had outgrown its quality; nor could the great writers of earth bear any message to the mind too undeveloped to receive it. The 'Letters,' 'Gold Foil,' etc., are books peculiarly fitted to aspiring young people, in susceptible stages of mental development. To a thoughtful boy of a certain age they would be what Emerson would come to be to him five years later, and there is no gainsaying the good they have done." We are apt, in this electric age of thought, to turn superciliously from what we denominate the "goody-goody" style of writing; it quickly palls, and still the constant adherence to the fundamental principles of all true living is yet a thing to make all conscious life better, and a faith for whose abiding firmness we should be thankful. For in the crisis hours of life it is to the simple primitive virtues that we cling, after all. It is impossible for the critic of to-day rightly to judge these didactic works of Dr. Holland, unless he has in his own experience a knowledge of what, at a certain far-away epoch, they were to himself. "He touched commonplace lives to finer, nobler, issues." A farmer in one of our hill towns sought the sympathy and advice of his pastor, as his married life had not proved all he had hoped for, and at that special juncture the relations between himself and wife were greatly "strained," in fact he was contemplating separation. The pastor wisely declined to advise in a case where it was plain that both parties were to blame. A few days after he was driving by the field where the man was working. He at once came forward, and addressing the minister, said, "I've thought better of that matter I was talking to you about. Did you read Dr. Holland in Saturday's paper?" The minister replied that on Saturday he was too busy with his sermon for anything else. "Well, Holland was talking about how husbands and wives ought to treat each other, and I see I've been somewhat wrong myself, and I've made up my mind to stand by the woman, for better or for worse, till death do us part."

The success of these "Letters" was a great and inspiring recompense to a man who had worked hard and waited patiently, says Mr. Gladden, and when, a year later, he sent out "Gold Foil," he talked with his public in a straightforward but devoutly grateful spirit, as follows: "A few months ago the pen that traces these lines commenced a series of letters to the young. The letters accumulated and grew into a book; and this book, with honest aims and modest pretensions, has a place to-day in many thousand homes, while it has been read by hundreds and thousands of men and women in every part of our country. More and better than this, it has become an inspiring, moving, and directing power in a great aggregate of young life. I say this with that kind of gladness and gratitude which admits of little pride. I say it because it has been said to me—revealed to me in letters brimming with thankfulness and overflowing with friendliness; expressed to me in silent pressings of the hand—

pressings so full of meaning that I involuntarily looked at my palm to see if a jewel had not been left in it; uttered to me by eyes full of interest and pleasure; told me in plain and homely words, in the presence of tears that came unbidden. . . to vouch for their honesty. To say that all this makes me happy would not be to say all that I feel. I account the honor of occupying a pure place in the popular heart, of being welcomed in God's name into the affectionate confidence of those for whom life has high meanings and high issues, of being recognized as among the beneficent forces of society —the greatest honor to be worked for and won under the stars." This was the sort of satisfaction that some author "highly praised by the critics" had missed, when he said to Elizabeth Stuart Phelps, "I would crawl on my hands and knees till I sank, if I could write a book that the plain people would read and love."

CHAPTER V.

His First Novel, and the Beginning of his Lecturing Career
—"Bittersweet," "Miss Gilbert's Career," and the Civil
War—Eulogy on Lincoln.

OF course Dr. Holland's literary quality could not fail to make his book-notices and short editorial paragraphs attractive, and he had the sort of thoroughness that does whatever work is in hand as well as it possibly can be done; so that Mr. Bowles's boundless ability to gather news from every corner of the land and every walk in life, and Dr. Holland's editor's gift in dressing it in terse and vivacious language, produced a paper that people of differing political ideas would grumblingly buy, saying, "I don't take any stock in their politics, but I must have their paper."

While the Titcomb letters had been making their appearance he had produced and printed serially a novel, founded on early events in the history of Massachusetts, especially exhibiting the witchcraft delusion and some of its unhappy consequences. Incidentally it shows up some of the fallacies that dominated the Puritans, who while founding a col-

J. G. Holland
1860

ony whose ostensible corner-stone was freedom to worship God according to one's conscience, were cruelly intolerant toward religious opinions that did not exactly square with their own—a state of things that finally drove William Pynchon, one of the founders of Springfield, and a noble figure of a man, back to England to die after having given the flower of his days to the settlement, "because he had written a book in which he had given utterance to some opinions that were not considered orthodox by the authorities of Massachusetts Bay, though strict in the discharge of his magisterial, social, and Christian duties." That sentence, quoted from the "History of Western Massachusetts," contains the key to the attitude of Dr. Holland on doctrinal opinion and practical piety, and it was given him to discover that the New Englander's ability to take upon himself the direction of his neighbor's conscience and belief, had not altogether departed from him two hundred years later, when Dr. Holland himself was charged with heresy.

"Gold Foil" and "Letters to the Joneses" successively ran their course in the paper, and were duly gathered up and published by the Scribners, yielding a very comfortable royalty to the pocket of their author, and giving the distinction that comes to but few writers of any time—to be thought of with warm personal gratitude for some soul-help given when needed, some guiding light shot along some dark and dubious path. Go to the public libraries, ask for the books; their worn covers and be-thumbed and soiled pages, and the frequent rebinding, tell their own story of how they touch the popular heart. It is a not little interesting study of human nature to look through and note the "marked" passages, showing where he has spoken to the questionings and convictions of those inquiring souls, who will never cease to be while human lots and human lives are full of mysteries inexplicable.

It was at this period (1857) that Mr. Bowles made the brief experiment of conducting a newspaper in Boston; an enterprise that he ultimately found distasteful and abandoned. During his absence the conduct of the *Republican* was left entirely in Dr. Holland's hands—a work which he accomplished with signal ability, as testified in that paper's obituary notice of him.

This was the period of the greatest prosperity and usefulness of the village and town lyceums, before the lecture-bureau, with its tricks of trade and its sometimes mountebank performers, had blighted an incomparable agency for stimulating the intellectual life and elevating the moral standards of the masses. The human voice is certainly one of the most potent agencies through which God sends His various messages to man. One who was a very successful lecturer in that day, says: "Present visible personality, the nameless something we call magnetism, with a soul and a brain behind it, is, if not lasting, certainly the most absorbing and powerful influence to which masses of men and women ever have succumbed or ever will yield."

Among the thousands who had read Dr. Holland's books, there was a great curiosity to see their author and to hear him, as soon as they learned that he could speak acceptably. Invitations to lecture poured in upon him, especially from the West; in one season he spoke ninety times, and in talking about it he said, "The speaking is nothing, it is the travelling that kills. Engagements often wide apart, in regions where the travelling facilities are limited; in inclement weather, often missing connections and sometimes going to the lecture-hall hungry, having had time only to wash off the heaviest grime of the coal-dust; riding on an engine or hand-car, or in a farmer's very 'one-hoss' buggy; and after speaking, finding that, to be at all sure of reaching to-morrow's destination it would not answer to take the chances involved in a night's welcome rest, but I must take a bite and be off; still, through thick and through thin, and conquering all sorts of delays and difficulties, I never disappointed an audience." On one occasion, through an almost incredible lack of foresight on the part of a committee, he passed a whole twenty-four hours without a mouthful of food, and that not in the Western wilds, but in the near-by State of New Jersey.

He was a really eloquent speaker, and when he delivered his eulogy of Abraham Lincoln in the Springfield City Hall, in 1865, he won an oratorical triumph that surprised and delighted his most partial friends. His lecturing had brought him a goodly sum of money, so that he felt justified in adopting a refined and pleasant, though still modest, style of living, and he was rapidly realizing the dream of a home filled with all those adjuncts to true culture that had haunted his imagination from boyhood.

In 1858 he published his dramatic poem, "Bittersweet," of which ninety thousand copies have been sold, notwithstanding it was savagely attacked by some of the critics.

What now condenses itself into the phrase "the woman question," was then a cloud no bigger than a man's hand, but it could not escape the eye of such a moralist, *par excellence*, as he was; and in 1860 he put forth his novel—"Miss Gilbert's Career." Having in his own home one of the most womanly of women, and being a natural conservative, he took the view that woman's highest happiness is found at the fireside, and her truest work in the home. This was before the war had robbed more than half a million of women of any reasonable prospect of having firesides, and forced so many women to make the best they can of a second-rate style of happiness. One woman who knew him well says, "He did not entertain exhilarating views of woman's place in intellectual advancement, yet to the individual woman no one could be more tender, more helpful, more considerate." No one knew better than he the true value of that home-life which, it sometimes seems, needs to be rediscovered in this country. A man who knew him well said, "His domestic life was singularly beautiful and affectionate, his appreciation of all that is fine, and noble, and holy in the varied family relations, runs as a golden vein through all his works." In one of the darkest hours of our war, when the stoutest hearts were failing, he said in a lecture, "No nation can be destroyed while it possesses a good home-life. My lawn cannot be spoiled so long as the grass is green, no matter how many trees may be prostrated, no matter how many flowers may be trampled under feet by unclean beasts. The essential life and beauty of the lawn are in the grass and not in the trees, and not in the flowers, and not in any creature that passes over it; and the life of a nation is not in political institutions, and not in political parties, and not in politicians or great men, but in the love-inspired home-life of the people." He puts these words into the mouth of a character in one of his books. The man is talking of his home, and says, "It is resonant with little feet, and musical with the voices of children. They climb my knees when I return from the fatigues of the day. I walk in the garden with their little hands clinging to mine. I listen to their prayers at their mother's knee. I settle their petty disputes. I find in them and in their mother all the solace and satisfaction that I desire or need. Clubs cannot win me from their society. Fame, honor, place, have no charms to crowd them from my heart. My home is my rest, my amusement, my consolation, my treasure-house, my earthly heaven." It would have served for a picture of his own, and thus he writes of children, "Ah, this taking to one's arms a little group of souls fresh from the hand of God, and living with them in loving companionship, is, or ought to be, like living in heaven." The man who held those views is not exactly to blame for still thinking that the men could continue to do the necessary voting.

Then came the war. Before that time the daily circulation of the *Republican* was five thousand seven hundred; that of the weekly, eleven thousand two hundred and eighty; but who can describe the activity of the times when, as Dr. Holmes exhaustively said, "we found but two things were absolutely necessary—bread and the newspaper—and of course the newspaper as a mere vehicle for the latest intelligence from 'the front.'" It was Mr. Bowles's deciding voice which determined the general political course of the paper, but in the exciting years that immediately preceded the war, Dr. Holland had written many political articles, and had entered with great enthusiasm into the canvass that first sent the Hon. Henry L. Dawes to Congress; and it is easy to see how he would feel toward a system founded on a radical wrong. When John Brown was condemned, the *Republican* said: "Nobody can respect an institution to the safety of which the death of the too ardent lover of liberty is essential." Whether he penned the sentence or not, it is worthy of representing the natural attitude his mind would take in viewing the event.

In a lecture delivered toward the close of the war, he said: "Patriotism is simple and trustful like family affection; and its subordinate place in the ordinary life of the nation is seen in the fact that it rarely shows itself except in the national emergencies. When the country is endangered, or insulted, or outraged, then we learn something of the strength and the universality of patriotism, and then we learn something of its inspiring and motive power in national action. . . . The voice of that first hostile cannon turned against the flag that floated over Fort

Sumter reached the national heart; and the nation casting off every fetter stood up as one man, and called for vengeance. . . . I know of nothing more sublime than this sudden waking of a nation through an outrage upon the object of its love."

After the four years of struggle, losses, and sacrifices were over, the assassination of Mr. Lincoln sent a thrill of horror through the North and made every man in it a mourner. On the day of the funeral in Washington, similar services were held throughout the North, and Dr. Holland was asked to deliver a eulogy in the City Hall of Springfield. In this effort his powers of oratory seem to have attained their apotheosis, if we may judge of the effect produced as described by eye-witnesses. The audience itself was highly sympathetic and responsive; if the "prosperity of a jest lies in the ear of him that hears it," how much more would a funeral address appeal to the keenest sensibilities of an audience solemnized and exalted to the highest degree. Remembering Dr. Holland's deeply religious nature, and his firm belief that Lincoln had been developed by the providence of God, for the work he had done, in a manner which no other or different man could have done; and also Lincoln's own unshakable faith that God was overruling all events so that right and justice should finally triumph, and the solemn fervor with which, in his public utterances, he prayed for guidance and gave thanks for successes, we are not surprised that Dr. Holland laid great stress on the religious side of Mr. Lincoln's character. All through the war he had tenaciously held to the theory that it was a great mercy to our country, that no man of supreme military and statesmanlike genius—no Cæsar or Napoleon—had risen among us, that the great struggle had been carried to a successful conclusion by "an average American," and that heart and conscience had been higher factors in the safe working out of our problem than dazzling intellectual gifts.

Here is his estimate of the man, and considering the blinding halo of martyrdom that, at the moment, surrounded the figure of the dead President, it is cool, clear, and just. "Strong without greatness, acute without brilliancy, penetrating but not profound, he was in intellect an average American in the walk of life in which the nation found him. He was loved for the qualities of heart and character which I have attributed to him, and not those powers and that culture which distinguish the majority of our eminent men. In the light of these facts, let us look for a moment at what this simple-hearted, loving, honest Christian man has done. Without an extraordinary intellect, without the training of the schools, without a wide and generous culture, without experience, without the love of two-thirds of the nation, without an army or a navy at the beginning, he has presided over and guided to a successful issue the most gigantic struggle that the history of the world records. He has called to his aid the best men of the time, without a jealous thought that they might overshadow him; he has managed to control their jealousies of each other and compelled them to work harmoniously; he has sifted out from weak and infected material men worthy to command our armies and lead them to victory; he has harmonized conflicting claims, interests, and policies; and in four years has absolutely annihilated the military power of a rebellion thirty years in preparation, and having in its armies the whole military population of a third of the republic, and at its back the entire resources of the men in arms and the producing power of four million slaves. Before he died he saw the rebellion in the last throes of dissolution, and knew that his great work was accomplished. . . . He found the nation weak and tottering to destruction. He left it strong—feared and respected by the nations of the world. He found it full of personal enemies; he leaves it with such multitudes of friends that no one, except at personal peril, dares to insult his memory. Through the long nights of peril and of sorrow, of faithlessness and of fear, he has led us into a certain peace—the peace for which we have labored and prayed and bled for these long, long years. . . . I should be false to you, false to the occasion, false to the memory of him we mourn, and false to the God he worshipped and obeyed, if I should fail to adjure you to remember that all our national triumphs of law and humanity over rebellion and barbarism, have been won through the wisdom and power of a simple, honest, Christian heart. . . . What Mr. Lincoln achieved, he achieved for us ; but he left as choice a legacy in his Christian example, in his incorruptible integrity, and in his unaffected simplicity, if we will appropriate it, as in public deeds. . . . I can never think of that toil-worn man, rising long before his household and spending an hour with his Maker and his Bible, without tears. In that silent hour of communion, he has drawn from the fountain which has fed all these qualities that have so won upon our faith and love. There, day after day, while we have been sleeping, he has knelt and prayed for us, prayed for the country, prayed for victory, prayed for wisdom and guidance, prayed for strength for his great mission, prayed for the accomplishment of his great purposes. There has he found consolation in trial, comfort in defeat and disaster, patience in reverses, courage for labor, wisdom in perplexity, and peace in the consciousness of God's approval. . . . Why should we not love him as we have loved no other chief magistrate? He was a consecrated man, consecrated to his country and his God!" These excerpts give but a faint notion of the power and pathos of an address which was listened to with intense and often tearful attention; they are selected to show what Dr. Holland believed were the mainsprings in the life and character of Abraham Lincoln.

CHAPTER VI.

Undertakes the "Life of Lincoln"—Complete Harmony
with his Subject—View of Lincoln's Essential Traits—
His Religious Side and Deep Melancholy.

THE address led up to a fresh chapter of success in the life of Dr. Holland. At that time very little was known of the life of this remarkable man, who had appeared at a crisis in the history of the nation, out of comparative obscurity, and had proved miraculously equal to the occasion, except what had been learned from his public acts. There was an eager curiosity to learn of his early days, and of the antecedents of this phenomenal career. An enterprising publisher saw his chance, asked Dr. Holland to do the work, and at once he was speeding westward to gather up the smallest fragments of information. Completed within the space of a few months, but condensing and combining all the facts then obtainable—for it must be remembered that the immense mass of public archives since availed of by Lincoln's biographers were then inaccessible—it was an interesting, readable, popular, essentially journalistic biography ; possessing among its elements that greatest of all—timeliness; reaching a sale in a very short time of nearly one hundred thousand copies, and, to use his own words, inuring so greatly to his financial benefit, "that I felt I might carry out some objects that had always been very near my heart."

The death of Mr. Lincoln had by no means quenched party feeling, or extinguished political animosities, and in his preface Dr. Holland said: "I have not attempted to disguise or conceal my own personal partiality for Mr. Lincoln, and my thorough sympathy with the political principles to which his life was devoted. Though unconscious of any partiality for a party capable of blinding my vision, or distorting my judgment, I am aware that, at this early day, when opinions are still sharply divided upon the same questions concerning principles, policies, and men which prevailed during Mr. Lincoln's active political life, it is impossible to utter any judgment which will not have a bearing upon the party politics of the time. Thus, the only alternative of writing according to personal partialities and personal convictions, has been writing without any partialities, and without any convictions. I have chosen to be a man, rather than a machine; and if this shall subject me to the charge of writing in the interest of a party, I must take what comes of it.

"I have tried to paint the character of Mr. Lincoln

and to sketch his life, clinging closely by his side. . . . to throw light upon specially interesting phases of his private life and public career, to exhibit the style and scope of his genius, and to expose his social, political, and religious sentiments and opinions."

The early trials of Dr. Holland fitted him to enter into the life of the son of the poverty-stricken pioneer with fullest insight. Thomas Lincoln was one of the "rolling-stones," and Dr. Holland very incisively says: "When inefficient men become very uncomfortable, they are quite likely to try emigration as a remedy. A good deal of what is 'the pioneer spirit' is simply a spirit of shiftless discontent." The poor little home which it had cost infinite toil to establish was sold for ten barrels of whiskey—bought to be bartered in the new locality—and twenty dollars in money. It was left behind, but not till the mother had taken her living boy with her to pay a last visit to the grave of the little son she had buried; an incident never forgotten by her illustrious son. The new home was poorer and more destitute of comforts than the old one, and the mother could no longer withstand the hardships and deprivations of border life; and when Abraham was ten years old she died of quick consumption, and was laid to rest under the trees near the lonely cabin, with none but the simplest ceremonies. "But neither father nor son was content to part with her without a formal Christian tribute to her worth and memory. For many years Abraham Lincoln never saw a church, but there came to the poor home in Kentucky, at intervals of several months, one of those faithful, humble, itinerant preachers whose influence for good in inchoate American communities can never be measured, named Elkin—a Baptist—to which church Thomas and Nancy Lincoln belonged." From him Abraham Lincoln gained his first notion of public speaking, and he remembered him with admiring love. The father could not write, but the boy had, by snatches and under three different teachers—in all being at school less than a year—acquired an imperfect but legible penmanship, his copy-book being often the sand at his feet, or a bit of birch-bark. So father and son united in a letter describing the mother's death, and asking him to come to Indiana and preach her funeral sermon. To comply would require the poor preacher to ride on horseback nearly a hundred miles through the wilderness, "and it is certainly to be remembered, to the humble itinerant's honor, that he was willing to pay this tribute of respect to the woman who had so thoroughly honored him and his sacred office." He answered the letter, appointing a future Sunday when he would come, and commissioned the young writer to notify the neighbors, little dreaming that his kind act would find remembrance wherever the life-history of the martyr-President is read or known. The people came from twenty miles around, and those who sit at ease and asleep in Zion, ought to read Dr. Holland's account of the gathering, to learn what "gospel privileges" mean to those who are not saturated with them. The good parson preached with unusual fluency and fervor, and spoke of the precious Christian woman who had gone with the warm praise she deserved, and held her up as an example of true womanhood.

"Those who knew the tender and reverent spirit of Abraham Lincoln later in life, will not doubt that he returned to his cabin-home deeply impressed by all that he had heard. It was the rounding-up for him of a Christian mother's life and teachings. It recalled her sweet and patient example, her assiduous efforts to inspire him with pure and noble motives, her simple instructions in divine truth, her devoted love for him, and the motherly offices she had rendered him during all his tender years. His character was planted in this Christian mother's love; and those who have wondered at the truthfulness and earnestness of his mature character, have only to remember that the tree was true to the soil from which it sprang." Mr. Lincoln always looked back to her with an unspeakable affection, and long after, said to a friend, "All that I am or hope to be,

I owe to my angel mother." The tribute to Christian character would have been equally true of Dr. Holland's mother's, with the difference that he was able to do all that mortal affection and assiduity could do to make her happy long after his career had been crowned with success.

The more Dr. Holland learned of Lincoln's character and career, the more deeply was he impressed with the essentially religious elements that were at their foundation, and his carefully elaborated statement of it becomes interesting when compared with his own carefully expressed views, whenever he had deemed that any good could be effected by such an expression. He says: "He was a religious man. The fact may be stated without any reservation, with only an explanation. He believed in God and in His personal supervision of the affairs of men. He believed himself to be under His control and guidance. He believed in the power and ultimate triumph of the right through his belief in God. This unwavering faith in a Divine Providence began at his mother's knee and ran like a thread of gold through all the inner experiences of his life. His constant sense of human duty was one of the forms by which his faith manifested itself. His conscience took a broader grasp than the simple apprehension of right and wrong. He recognized an immediate relation between God and himself in all the actions and passions of his life. He was not 'professedly' a Christian—that is, he subscribed to no creed, joined no organization of Christian disciples. He spoke little then (when a young man), perhaps less than he did afterward, and always sparingly, of his religious belief and experiences; but that he had a deep religious life, sometimes imbued with superstition, there is no doubt. We guess at a mountain of marble by the outcropping ledges that hide their whiteness among the ferns."

Many people fail to realize what a deep and abiding hold anti-slavery views had upon the man who was to go down in history as the emancipator of four millions of slaves, even when a very young statesman and when he was very lonesome in holding them. In the year 1836, when Lincoln was twenty-seven, he was a member of the Legislature of Illinois from Sangamon County, and he and his fellow-member from the same county—whom we are justified in fancying might be influenced by a man of Mr. Lincoln's great argumentative powers— were the only two who would sign a protest that "the institution of slavery is founded on both injustice and bad policy." This was the beginning of Mr. Lincoln's anti-slavery record, which culminated, twenty-six years after, in the Emancipation Proclamation. The sublimest moment in the history of that epoch-making document was the one in which

Mr. Lincoln informed his cabinet of his unalterable determination to issue it; because, said Mr. Lincoln, "I have promised my God that I will do it;" and when Mr. Chase asked if he had heard correctly, Mr. Lincoln replied: "I made a solemn vow before God that, if General Lee should be driven back from Pennsylvania, I would crown the result by the declaration of freedom to the slaves." Two days after, in alluding to the proclamation, when a large body of men had appeared before the White House in recognition of it, he said: "What I did, I did after a very full deliberation, and under a heavy and solemn sense of responsibility. I can only trust in God I have made no mistake." Two years later he was able to say: "As affairs have turned, it is the central act of my administration, and the great event of the nineteenth century."

A lady, in writing to Professor John Fiske, asked him whether he discerned what the old divines used to call "The hand of God in history." This is his reply: "I am sure that I do. My *belief* that all human life is the working out of a Divine Idea, to be realized in God's own good time, is as unshakable as my belief in my own existence. But for this belief, the study of history would have no interest for me."

Certainly Dr. Holland was greatly capable of entering into the motives of a man who had this deep abiding sense of God's direction of the whirlwind of war, and it is no wonder that the book, which was a marvel of rapid work, met a ready sale and helped to enthrone Lincoln in some hearts that had but reluctantly yielded their allegiance. He did not blink the blemishes in the grand character —he accounted for them by exhibiting the coarse and meagre surroundings of the hard pioneer life.

People have sometimes wondered that a work so hastily written should have attained so great a popularity; but the subject, of whose early life, at that time, very little was known, the historian, and the eager audience to which the recital was addressed, all had, deep down, the religious element in common. Lincoln regarded himself as a man of destiny —he did not look upon himself as an aimless atom floating on a "stream of tendency," but—certainly after the war began—as God-appointed to carry it forward—an agent set apart for a peculiar work— just as irrevocably dedicated to it as David was to his by Samuel's anointing. Into this spirit his biographer could heartily enter, as well as into the melancholy produced by seeing the terrible destruction of heart, and hope, and health, and life, and home, wrought by the war. It was little wonder in 1862, in the midst of reverses, that Mr. Lincoln should say, "I shall never be glad any more;" and certainly, as the responsibilities and fatigues of the struggle made deeper inroads upon his strength and vitality, the presentiment took possession of him that he should not survive its completion. We may call it superstition, or fanaticism, but it is none the less certain that Mr. Lincoln for years dwelt in the shadow of Azrael's wing, and that it tinged with deep solemnity both his acts and his public utterances. One needs to have grown up in the shadow of New England theology, as preached and believed in, in Dr. Holland's early manhood, to appreciate what a preparation was his for entering into the very structure and attitude of Mr. Lincoln's mind. And as to the public he addressed, had they not seen, like the Israelites, "the horse and his rider overthrown," and a people emerging in victory and triumph from the bloody sea through which they had passed, under the captaincy of this fore-ordained leader? Subject, biographer, and public were alike suited to each other, and therein lies the secret of the phenomenal success.

No one felt more than Dr. Holland himself the imperfections that must inhere in such a hastily gathered book. He says in his preface: "The humble biographers of Mr. Lincoln, though they satisfy an immediate want and gather much that would, otherwise, be forever lost, can hardly hope to be more than tributaries to that better and complete biography which the next, or some succeeding, generation will be sure to produce and possess." "The life of Washington, even though it was written by a Marshall, . . . waited half a century to give it symmetry and completeness." Certainly one can be too near a period, or a man, to give either a just historical perspective ; but posterity will be grateful to Dr. Holland for his sympathetic story of a wonderful life, lived in the midst of events that will go down in history as a marvellous example of what can be accomplished by "a government of the people, by the people, and for the people."

CHAPTER VII.

Becomes the Possessor of "Brightwood"—A Pioneer in Domestic Sanitation—Publication of "Kathrina"—Invited to Edit *Hours at Home*—European Sojourn—Founding of *Scribner's Monthly*—Death of Mr. Scribner—Illustrations of the Magazine—Pride in his Lay Pulpit.

As the work of Dr. Holland became more exclusively literary, he did more and more of it at home, in his own library; there he wrote most of his book-notices, which were trenchant and interesting, and very good guides to the worth or worthlessness of books, as adapted to the mental and moral needs of those average New England men and women who were the readers of the *Republican*.

The pecuniary success of his lecture-tours and his books had been such, that at last he felt warranted in indulging in one of the prime pleasures of a man of taste—building a house according to his own ideas. After he had done that "best day's work for himself," in marrying Miss Chapin, he and his wife lived with her widowed mother; but without making any special ado in the matter, and blowing a trumpet of discovery, Dr. Holland had thought out for himself a system of prophylactic hygiene, especially as related to those who had reason to suppose they were predisposed to pulmonary consumption. It was thoroughly original with him, and in advance of his time—for the now familiar inquiries in regard to the relation of soil-moisture to this disease, had not then been initiated—and the much-instructed public of to-day has not yet caught up with his positions; and if he was ever inclined to mourn over having spent so many years in striving to fit himself for a profession that was to be eventually laid aside, he ought to have been reconciled, by realizing that it had given him just ideas as to what goes to the building of a healthy body. At that time nobody thought of actively combating a consumptive tendency—its infectiousness had not been dreamed of—and where one or more members of a family had been swept off by it, the wiseacres shook their heads and said, "It's only a question of time as to when the rest will go." Two of the Doctor's sisters had died of it, within the compass of a year, and a third had followed in a month or two with measles.

There were circumstances connected with the death of the last sister, that preyed deeply on his mind, and this, added to the overwork of the struggle to become educated, and earn the needful money at the same time, had produced in him a physical condition far different from what he exhibited in the later time of his robust and vigorous manhood. The upheaval of opinion that had invaded the world of traditional religion had also attacked hoary beliefs in medicine, the air was full of therapeutic "isms" and "pathies," but in the midst of the ferment it was being found out that disease, instead of being a distinct entity, that you could kill with a poison, or let out with a lancet—as you would wring a chicken's neck and have done with it—consisted in a lack of balance and completeness in the processes that go to the building up of the system, some hinderance to the perfect performance of the vital functions. Long before it had been proved that dry soil for a house to stand on, and consequent dry air above it for its inmates to breathe, is a fundamental condition in preventing the development of the seeds of consumption, Dr. Holland had made up his mind that he would forsake the damp river bank, and so he selected a house on a sandy spot, on which pine-trees readily grew. As it was not a "fashionable" locality, the remark was made "Who ever would want to live there, except some hare-brained poet like Dr. Holland?" notwithstanding which remark, his family and himself lived there and thrived. Undoubtedly, the relief from worry that came with his finding his true vocation in congenial and steady employment, contributed its share,

THE BUFF COTTAGE
[Where "Bittersweet" was written]

and the greater ease in commanding the elements of good living that came in with railroads, helped. Certain it is, that after an interval of being "delicate" —the word then used to describe a lack of robust health—he developed a constitution that bore the wear and tear of editorial life, and the exhausting work of the lecturer, for many years, without a thought that he was not physically fully up to par. He was a striking example of what intelligent and rational living can do.

But the modest little "Buff Cottage," in which he had grown into a recognized position among forces that were moulding his region and his day, was small, his daughters were growing up, and the yearning to create a home in accordance with his own ideas took possession of him, and he built "Brightwood"—a house in which he incorporated some novel notions, especially in the brilliant coloring, of which it was the first example in the vicinity, but which is now so much used as to be commonplace. This again was so radically unique, that people said, "Just what you'd expect in one of these literary men;" but instead of its being one of those daring innovations that nobody would follow, it showed him in touch with the spirit of his time, and that while travelling up and down the land he had kept his eyes and ears open, and knew that the next evolution in thought would be the æsthetic. In the grounds about the house there was room for the embodiment of all his dreams—the carefully kept lawn, the pleasant brook, the rustic bridges—in short all that makes a "place" befitting the gentleman; and earth probably has few deeper joys than that which he felt on taking possession of this charming home, won by his own indefatigable industry. Here were gathered the three elements which Beecher says are indispensible to a true home—age, middle life, and childhood. One of the fairest chambers was devoted to the still living, sad-hearted mother; there were charming apartments for the two daughters, and all that could make the nursery perfect for the baby boy. The parlor walls bore evidences that he felt he might indulge in an occasional good picture.

At that date he might have been cited as the most successful man of letters in the United States, measured either by the number of his readers or by the solid pecuniary rewards that had come to him. In commenting upon the almost reckless generosity with which he extended help to the needy, especially if they were fellow-wielders of the pen, one man, who knew him, says, " He was, notwithstanding, a methodical and careful man of business, and seldom one man combines the two qualities of thrift and generosity to the same extent." Perhaps part of the explanation of the husbanding of the resources that had mainly been fished up out of an inkstand, so that they could be constructed into an attractive, modern, æsthetic home, lies in a direction indicated in the experience of a minister, who found it very hard to resist the spending of money, and so, as quickly as possible, passed all of his receipts into the hands of his wife, saying, "She's the only one of this pair that has a particle of saving grace."

In 1867 he published "Kathrina," and it rapidly reached a sale of one hundred thousand copies— and to this day has a steady sale. It will long be prized for its accurate delineations of the ideas that pervaded the mind of ante-railroad Central New England sixty years ago, while it yet remained a secluded and homogeneous section, whose very foundations had been laid in such strong demarcation in theological opinions as constituted the holders of them a peculiar people without their knowing or suspecting it.

Seventeen years he had worked—cheerfully, industriously, and unremittingly—in the editorial harness of a daily paper, for his books and lectures were literal asides from the main labor of his life. Already he had been urged to come to New York and take charge of a magazine—*Hours at Home*—then published by the Scribner firm, the scope of which needed broadening to meet the demands of the time; but his daughters were just leaving school, and he felt that he had earned a rest, and so had the faithful, energetic, careful wife, and a foreign tour presented itself to him in an irresistible aspect. It had always been his delight to lavish on his children all the wealth of opportunity that had been denied to his own youth.

His connection with the *Republican* was brought to a close in 1867. Brightwood was rented, and he set forth on a pilgrimage which was to broaden his mind, develop his æsthetic taste, increase his acquaintance with universal human nature, and fit him worthily to occupy the lofty niche of pure and uplifting influence then preparing for him. He believed that the European trip was a Providential preparation for the larger field.

It happened that President Porter, of Yale College, who had been Dr. Holland's first pastor—he had united with the church by letter—when he came an unknown physician to try to make a place for himself in Springfield, was a guest at Brightwood on the night before the family left for their tour. The pastor had sympathized with the young man in his struggle with poverty and obscurity, against what seemed unconquerable odds, and could fully appreciate the contrast presented by the life in this beautiful home, and those days of darkness; and certainly it was a truly American antithesis of circumstances that this proud-spirited man, who had winced under the rebukes of a superintendent of a cotton-mill for careless work, should be able to entertain in a fitting manner the president of a leading college as his peer. But not of this was he thinking as the household knelt for their morning worship, a habit which Dr. Holland always maintained. President Porter says: "The doctor offered a singularly fervent and characteristic prayer of thanksgiving and praise for the blessings of his life in that house, in which he seemed to pass that portion of his life in review, in most heartfelt gratitude for the way, guidance, and blessing of God."

Unwittingly to those concerned this was "Finis" to a completed chapter of life; when they set forth it was the closing of a gate on the road passed over, for when they returned to it, it was merely pausing at a station, before pressing on to new regions.

He was resolved that the European trip should be something more than a mere arriving at places, and rushing through dozens of cathedrals, and past miles of pictures and statues; that it should, if possible, result in a culture that should "strike in," and not be a mere surface polish. Sojourns of greater or lesser length were made in places that could supply superior instructors to his daughters in music and languages. Himself he confessed "too old to learn a foreign tongue"—a happy circumstance those will think who regard his simple, pure, idiomatic English the best possible of all languages in which *his* message could be conveyed to his audience. He applied his powers of observation and comparison to the study of men, and current events, with all his wonted keenness and diligence, and it is refreshing in these days of flickering patriotism, and Anglomania in influential quarters, that he came back singing louder pæans than ever that God had hidden America till the fulness of time, and then had developed a country where any one of those that Burns describes as a man, who is a man "for a' that and a' that," could find work and a home. While the daughters were studying music, and the little boy was absorbing foreign tongues from his instructors, a trouble that had long been latent in Mrs. Holland's eyes took on a new and active form that necessitated treatment at the hands of the celebrated Von Gräfe, who did his best, but had to tell her that henceforth her vision would be greatly diminished—a limitation that called out afresh all the tenderness and chivalry in the nature of him who was pledged to care for her in sickness and in health, and the quiet bravery with which the deprivation was submitted to by Mrs. Holland, it seems, could have been shown only by a woman whose "heart was stayed on God."

At the end of two years they came back, and very soon after, as the writer was passing from Pittsfield to Springfield, Dr. Holland came into the car at Russell. After the exchange of hearty greetings, for we had long been friendly, I said, "Tell me about Europe." "Oh, splendid, beautiful, but I was tired to death of loafing, and longed to be at work again," and then he proceeded to tell how that when he went away an offer to edit a magazine—*Hours at Home*—then published by Scribner, had been made, and that it had remained open during his absence. He dwelt on the beauty and nobility of Mr. Scribner's character, which through many years he had had an opportunity to study. He dwelt on his purity of soul and loftiness of aim; "he would never lend his sanction to anything of doubtful moral quality." He kindled a high admiration for Mr. Scribner in his listener, and then added, "I had lots of time to think, and I fully made up my mind that there was a field for a new literary magazine in America."

Previously to going to Europe he had made the acquaintance of Mr. Roswell Smith, then a lawyer of Indiana, and had formed a high opinion of Mr. Smith's acute business judgment and great business ability. They met again in Europe, and discussed, among other things, the proposition as to the editorship of *Hours at Home*—a proposition that, while it offered a field, presented no dominating attraction to the doctor. In his own account of the founding of Scribner's new magazine he says, "I had concluded that there was no such thing as a great success for that magazine; that I did not myself like it, and that I would not identify myself with it, or tie myself to its traditions." Mr. Smith, on account of his health and for some other reasons, was desirous of coming East to live, and both of them were turning their eyes Americawards, and were ready to form definite plans for the future. They met on a bridge in Geneva, and the conversation at once reverted to the editorship, and, to cite Dr. Holland again: "When I said that instead of entering upon the editorship of an old magazine, I should like to start a new one, he [Mr. Smith] announced himself ready to undertake, as business manager, an enterprise of that kind with me. The result of the conversation . . . was a verbal agreement that we should unite our forces, on our return to America, for the effecting of this project." No wonder that that Geneva bridge thenceforth became a uniquely significant landmark in the lives of both these gentlemen. As Mr. Smith returned before Dr. Holland, he bore a letter of introduction to Mr. Charles Scribner, "commending him in such terms to the publisher's consideration and confidence as have been a thousand times justified by his subsequent business history." This was what Dr. Holland wrote when reviewing the phenomenally successful history of the magazine at the close of the eleven years when it exchanged the name, "*Scribner's*" for that of *The Century Magazine;* he also added, "As the inventors would say, 'I claim the discovery of Mr. Roswell Smith, and the combination with Mr. Charles Scribner and myself, which resulted in the production of *Scribner's Monthly.*'" Dr. Holland penned that sentence in June, 1881, at a time when there had been radical changes made in all the business relations among the proprietors of the magazine, but little suspected that it was to be as if with his own hand he had engraved the headstone, to mark the grave of *the* publication with which his life was identified; for this was written a little over three months previous to his death, and the second number of the newly christened *Century* was the one that announced that "Finis" had been written at the end of Dr. Holland's career, and contained in lieu of the familiar "Topics of the Time" his obituary notice.*

The plans of *Scribner's Monthly* were matured during the summer and autumn of 1870, the first number appearing in November. In order to place the magazine on an independent financial basis, and at the same time retain the benefit which came from a connection with the publishing house,

* The portion of the first edition that goes to foreign lands was already printed and on its way when he died, October 12, 1881.

a stock company was organized under the name of Scribner & Co., the parties to the plan becoming the stockholders.

If Dr. Johnson were moralizing on the situation he would exclaim: "Alas for the vanity of human expectations!" for in less that a year from the appearance of the first number the greatest of all circumstances that possibly could, did occur, in the untimely death of Mr. Scribner, as his charming personality was the focus of crystallization around which all the other elements arranged themselves. His sons succeeded to his pecuniary interests, and it was a tribute to the power of a noble name that, though he was dead, the magazine should still bear that name after having been carried to an almost unprecedented success by other hands than his. In the first number Dr. Holland said: "The privilege of selecting this title has been fraught with rare pleasure to the editor, for it has furnished to him the opportunity to honor one of the strongest personal friendships of his life, and to give befitting recognition to a name that, as the head of a large publishing house, has been associated for many years with what is purest and best in American literature. The magazine needs no higher aim than to be worthy of the name it bears, and can achieve no better honor than to do its part to maintain the position which the house represented by it holds before the Christian people of this country." *Scribner's Monthly* absorbed *Hours at Home, Putnam's*, and the *Riverside.* "It started," says Dr. Holland, " without a subscriber, but it is remarkable in reviewing its career that it never printed or sold less than forty thousand copies a month. The highest task we set ourselves in those early days was to reach an edition of one hundred thousand copies—a number now (1881) largely surpassed. That this success has been a surprise to the publishing fraternity is undoubtedly true; that two men, utterly unused to the business, should succeed from the first in so difficult a field, is, in the retrospect, a surprise to themselves."

Dr. Holland was accustomed to say of his life and the different positions he had filled, that he never had fitted himself beforehand for them; that he stepped in, and then worked with all his power to adapt himself to the place in which he found himself, and, stepping from the country newspaper to a position here at Scribner's, the editorial chair of a magazine that was soon to achieve an international reputation was no exception; but in reviewing its evolution he said: " Of the editorial management of *Scribner*, I have nothing to say except that it has been conscientiously and industriously performed, and that I have had a corps of able and enthusiastic assistants, who have given themselves to the work as if the magazine, indeed, were all their own." In weighing the value of the various elements that had built up the wonderful success he was perfectly just, and could he have known that four months later he was to die, his expressions of appreciation could not have been more deliberate and accurate. He did not claim the highest place for its literary contents, but said, "the success was owing to the superb engravings, and the era it had introduced of improved illustrated art." Everybody does not know how the pace set by the *Scribner* spurred other magazines to new endeavors, and led the way to rich monthly feasts, set before the public in pictures of all imaginable things in the skies and the air, in the earth and in the waters under the earth. Dr. Holland bestowed the praise where it was deserved: "This feature of our work is attributable to Mr. R. W. Gilder and to Mr. A. W. Drake—the former the office editor, and the latter superintendent of the illustrative department. Mr. Smith and I, any further than we have stood behind these men with encouragement and money, deserve no credit for the marvellous development that has been made in illustration. Perhaps this is not quite true, for Mr. Smith was the first to insist on the experiment of printing the illustrated forms on dry paper. This has had much to do with the success of our cuts, and the *Scribner's Monthly* enjoyed a practical mo-

HIS VIRTUAL VALEDICTORY 83

nopoly of this mode of cut-printing for years. The effects achieved in this way excited great curiosity, both in this country and in England. Mr. Smith may, therefore, legitimately claim to have revolutionized the cut-printing of the world; and it is another illustration of the fact that reforms are rarely made in their own art by routine men. It takes a mechanic to invent an agricultural machine; and a lawyer turned man of business to discover that damp paper is not the best for printing cuts on."

He then enters into an explanation of the business arrangements that were to control the magazine in future—he had now ceased to be a proprietor in the magazine—and events soon proved the wisdom of the action then taken, and the closing sentence of what he wrote proved to be his valedictory as to his connection with the magazine, for when he went, it was with no word of farewell, but with the ink still wet on a "Topic of the Time" lying unfinished on his desk. His near friends all knew that he lived with a sword suspended above his head, in the form of incurable heart disease. His own medical knowledge prevented his indulging in those "illusions of hope" that do so much to prolong life in many cases; but all the same he "marched breast forward," doing his daily task as faithfully as ever. He said: "With the burden of business responsibilities lifted from my shoulders, I hope to find my hand more easily at work with my pen, and trust that for many years I may hold the relation to the great reading world which this editorial position gives me. I risked in this business all the reputation and all the money I had made, and it is a great satisfaction that I did not miscalculate the resources of my business associate or my own."

In his first "Topic of the Time" he says: "The feature of illustrations has been adopted to meet a thoroughly pronounced popular demand for the pictorial representation of life and truth, and in the well-assured belief that there is no person, young or old, learned or illiterate, to whom it will be unwelcome. With this popular auxiliary we shall try to make a magazine that is intelligent on all living questions of morals and society, and to present something in every number that will interest and instruct every member of every family into which it shall have the good fortune to find its way."

Could his mother, who had never been quite reconciled to his not being a minister, have seen him installed in this lay pulpit from which forty thousand copies went out in the first number, and each of which, it is fair to reckon, was read by at least five persons, she might have been made to realize that God had led him to being a preacher in his own way—*the* way for this bustling but reading nineteenth century.

CHAPTER VIII.

Robert Collyer on the Success of *Scribner's Monthly*, and the quality of "Topics of the Time"—First Symptoms of Heart Disease — Character of his Editorial Contributions—Lessons from the Deaths of Fisk and Tweed—The Revised Version of the Bible—Dogmatic Theology.

REV. ROBERT COLLYER was at this time living in Chicago, and saw how the magazine "exactly hit" that city of young, live, and practical men, and he was also travelling about over wide reaches of our country lecturing, and came into close contact with the masses of upright and sturdy people who make up the bone and sinew of the land—and wherever he goes he finds out what the people read. He says, speaking of its editor: "Nobody else could have built up the *Scribner* as he did, making it fill a place uniquely adapted to the great mass of the American people. He 'preached' constantly, not because he said to himself 'Go to now, let us discourse on ethics and morals,' but simply because he poured out what was in his heart; he was a power in the land, and when you read an article of his it led you onward and upward toward the best you were capable of. No other man in this country could so touch the daily lives of the practical people—the great company of those who not only constitute the bone and sinew of the land but its influential mind and heart as well."

Some years after the establishment of the magazine Dr. Collyer himself came to New York to live, and soon became a valued friend and visitor to Dr. Holland's house. He says: "Nothing struck a stranger more than the beautiful eagerness of the man to be about the work God had set him to do"—and it was a great work he did in those "Topics of the Time." No less than four hundred of them did he write, and among them are many pungent sermonettes, which being founded on the eternal verities are just as well adapted to the case in this sinning and mistaking world to-day as ever; but many of the most forcible and valuable ones at the time were called out by events of the day, the phases of feeling which were produced by the events, no matter how absorbing at the moment, are past and forgotten, and reading them now is like looking at the sunset clouds, after the sun that has filled them with rosy and purple lights has gone below the horizon—the form is there, but the glow is gone. When John Leech died he left hundreds of the original cartoons of those pictures for *Punch* that had set the whole world laughing in their time, and art lovers thought they represented a fortune for his family, but when brought into the auction-room it turned out that some of them which had been most triumphant in their day fell perfectly flat; very intelligent people couldn't even recall the circumstances that had been, as it were, photographed in caustic and aqua-fortis, and the sale was a great failure.

Of course Dr. Holland spared no pains to make his magazine interesting and popular, and more than once in the course of his experience it was given him to know that most exquisite of editorial pleasures— the discovery of a new star in the firmament of genius—as George William Curtis has told us, the editor lives in a state of perpetual expectation that some writer of an altogether new and transcendent quality is going to bring his finished product to his own particular magazine; two of Dr. Holland's notable finds being Mrs. Burnett and George W. Cable. The beautiful Brightwood home in Springfield, of course, had to be given up—and not without many a pang did the transfer to the city accomplish itself. An opportunity offered to buy a house, not yet completed, in Park Avenue, and of course it could be finished and decorated just to the fancy of the occupant, and certainly a most attractive home it was, and thither came many of the gifted, not only among the writers of our own land, but from over the sea, to arrange for the publication of this or that promising article, and the gatherings of the many "contributors," and others of the literary and artistic people of New York that it was Dr. Holland's delight to invite to stated "receptions," will long be remembered by those who were so happy as to be part of them. In that home Dr. Holland drank deep of the cup of happiness. He continued to lecture occasionally, the escape from the city to more sparsely peopled regions being often a grateful change—and then, about four years before his death, came an attack of *angina*—not very severe, but enough to prove that mischief was already at work, and that thenceforth the man who had been capable of no end of work and endurance of hardship must walk cautiously, and, as Dr. Holmes says, "shade the lamp of life with the hand." To one friend he said at this time, "I've had my death-warrant read. You know the doctors tell me that if I should see my own house on fire I must not run one step." Without disturbing his family he quietly and at once put his business affairs in such order that instant death would not find him unprepared in that regard, and while his knowledge of medicine taught him that his was an ever progressive disease, he had the plank of hope, supplied by the fact that the progress is often very slow, to cling to still. The calm courage with which he lived through those four industrious and fruitful

years came about as near to the moral sublime as it is ever given to mortals to exhibit or to witness. It might be supposed that this living face to face with death would project a sombre shade into his writings, but a sense of moral responsibility was the great abiding element of his life, and his inmost conviction was that the right living of the "life that now is" makes the best preparation for that which is to come—be it nearer or more distant—so that no intimation of added solemnity can anywhere be found.

In the very first volume of the magazine we find him treating, among other things, of "A Growing Vice of Business," "Professional Morality," "The Temperance Question and the Press." He was uncompromising on this question, and held that it was the duty of the press to teach temperance. He well knew that he would be called a "prig," and "righteous overmuch," but it did not deter him from giving full expression to his convictions, which had been deepened in those wine-growing countries that we have sometimes been told hold a perpetual prophylactic against drunkenness in the constant universal use of wine. His observations convinced him of the fallacy of this notion, and even if his preconceived ideas had proved true there, he was convinced that there was a radical climatic difference in the two continents, and said: "Our sparkling, sunny atmosphere, and the myriad incentives to hope and enterprise in our circumstances are stimulants of God's own appointment for the American people. This pouring down of intoxicating liquors is ten thousand times worse than waste—it is essential sacrilege. This straining of the nerves, this heating of the blood, this stimulation or stupefaction of the mind, this imposition of cruel burdens upon the digestive organs, is a foul wrong upon Nature. Tens of thousands of valuable lives are sacrificed every year to this Moloch of strong drink. The crime, the beggary, the disgrace, the sorrow, the disappointment, the disaster, the sickness, the death, that have flowed in one uninterrupted stream from the bottle and the barrel, throughout the length of the land, are enough to make all thinking and manly men curse their source and swear eternal enmity to it. . . . O Heaven! for one generation of clean and unpolluted men; men whose veins are not fed with fire; . . . men who do not stumble upon the rock of apoplexy at mid age, or go blindly groping and staggering down into a drunkard's grave, but who can sit and look upon the faces of their grandchildren with eyes undimmed and hearts uncankered. Such a generation as this is possible in America; and to produce such a generation as this the persistent, conscientious work of the public press is entirely competent as an instrumentality. *The press can do what it will;* and if it will faithfully do its duty Maine laws will come to be things unthought of, and temperance reformers and temperance organizations will become extinct."

A little later the murder of James Fisk, Jr., regarded as a martyrdom by his admirers, kindled a sort of glamour about a career essentially abhorrent to the moral sense, and young men talked as if they thought the violent and untimely end had in some way atoned for the corrupt and godless life. He cautioned his readers against the feeling that Fisk was any better man because he had been killed, and said, "No man ever died a more natural death than James Fisk, Jr., excepting perhaps Judas Iscariot. . . . When a man pushes his personality so far to the front of aggressive and impertinent schemes of iniquity as Fisk did, it is the most natural thing in the world for him to run against something that will hurt him, for dangers stand thick as malice and revenge can plant them in the path of godlessness and brutality. It is not to be denied that a pretty universal execration of this man's memory has been saved to him through the bloody mercy of a murderer ; . . . but Fisk is certainly none the better for having been killed. He was a bad man—bold and shameless and vulgar in his badness—with whom no gentleman could come in contact without a sense of degradation. . . ." In the same "Topic" of "Easy Lessons from Hard Lives" he referred to the downfall of Tweed and said: "Let every man who wields a pen or has an audience with the public do what he can to counteract the poisonous effects of these lives on the young, by calling attention to the fact that these men have simply met the fate of eminent rascality. Honesty *is* the best policy. Virtue *does* pay. Purity *is* profitable. Truthfulness and trustworthiness *are* infinitely better than basely won gold. A good conscience *is* a choicer possession than power. When those men were dazzling the multitude with their shows and splendors they knew that the world they lived in was unsubstantial; and we have no question that they expected and constantly dreaded the day of discovery and retribution."

In the very last magazine that contained the "Topics," he was recommending courses of instruction in political economy in our colleges, and commenting on "Literary Eccentricity," so that we know he did not feel the shadow of death although he knew it touched him.

In looking back through these "Topics," it is interesting to note how much in advance of his time he was on the questions that are agitating the professedly Christian people of the land, although he did not use the peculiar jargon that at present smites our ears, of "inerrancy," "higher criticism," "preterition," and the like. It may be said that he had thought clear through these questions for himself, and had come to solid conclusions; conclusions that no amount of ridicule or obloquy could induce him to forsake, and conclusions that he would not desist from proclaiming with voice and with pen. He is writing of the Revised Version of the New Testament, just then completed, and of which enormous numbers had been sold in England, notwithstanding which it was said that it was making little headway among the people. He thought it very difficult to learn whether this last statement was really true, but he said : "There are several classes which will naturally oppose the reception of the revision, both in this country and in England, and it is well to take account of them. The conservative naturally dislikes change and innovation. It does not matter from what quarter change may come, nor to what it may relate, he will oppose it; this class will oppose the revision as a matter of course. They prefer their truth in the old form, and the new form will be offensive to them. . . . There is a class of ignorant people to whom the King James version of the Bible is the inspired word of God in all its language. They regard a revision as a tampering with the sacred text, and as an essential profanation. The forms of language in which sacred truth has been presented to them are quite as sacred as the truth itself. These people cannot be reasoned with because they do not know enough to use their reason. To this class belonged the bigoted fool who declared that the new revision would make more infidels than all the Bob Ingersolls in the world, simply by its admissions that there had been some mistakes in the English Bible hitherto preached to the world. The unchristian dishonesty of such an attitude as this is only equalled by its foolishness. We fear that there is a leaven of this kind of dishonesty pretty widely scattered throughout the church—a feeling, or a fear, at least, that the exact truth in a new revision will remove some of the props from under old dogmas that had become precious, or that are regarded as fundamental in their accepted schemes of belief. Some of these people make a sort of fetich of the Bible. They carry it in their pockets as a sort of charm. No heathen ever gave the objects of his worship more superstitious reverence than these ignorant Christians do the Bible. Of course they would oppose any change in it.

". . . It is impossible that with the great advance of knowledge relating to the original Greek text that has been made since the King James version, . . . the new revision should not be better than the old. This should settle the question of universal acceptance ; it is the best thing we have.

"We should all remember that there is only one thing sacred about the Bible, viz., the truth that is in it. The language is the vehicle in or through which the truth is conveyed to our minds, and that version is best which most faithfully and forcibly conveys that truth. It would be a real benefit to Christendom to break up the idea that there is anything sacred and not to be touched in the language of the old English Bible, to kill out the reverence for the old forms in which truth has been conveyed." That was written six years before "Robert Elsmere" took his devastating iconoclasm among the English-speaking peoples of the world.

Dr. Holland gave his estimate of that "Dogmatic Theology" that has blighted the happiness out of thousands of innocent lives, in a "Topic" on "Preachers and Preaching"—he is talking of the *power of the affirmative*, and says, "A man who spends his days in arresting and knocking down lies and liars will have no time left for speaking the truth. . . . The author of Christianity understood this matter. His system of religion was to be preached, proclaimed, promulgated. Its friends were not to win their triumphs by denying the denials of infidelity, but by persistently affirming, explaining, and applying the truth. . . . The world has never discovered anything nutritious in a negation, and the men of faith and conviction will always find a multitude eager for the food they bear. Men will continue to drink from the brooks and refuse to eat the stones that obstruct them. . . . So the modern preacher preaches more and argues less. He declares, promulgates, explains, advises, exhorts, appeals. He does more than this. Instead of regarding Christianity solely as a scheme of belief and faith, and thus becoming the narrow expounder of a creed, he broadens into a critic and cultivator of human motive and character. We do not assert that modern preaching is entirely released from its old narrowness. There are still too many who heat over the old broth and ladle it out in the old way which they learned in the seminary. The 'preaching of Jesus Christ' is still, to multitudes, the preaching of a scheme of religion, the explanation of a plan, the promulgation of dogmata. . . . The man who preaches Christ the most effectively and acceptably to-day is he who tries all motive and character and life by the divine standard, who applies the divine life to the every-day life of the world, and whose grand endeavor is not so much to save men as to make them worth saving. He denounces wrong in public and private life; he exposes and reproves the sins of society; he applies and urges the motives to purity, sobriety, honesty, charity, and good neighborhood; he shows men to themselves; and then shows them the mode by which they may correct themselves. In all this he meets with wonderful acceptance, and, most frequently, in direct proportion to his faithfulness. . . . The world has come to the comprehension of the fact that, after all that may be said of dogmatic Christianity, *character* is the final result at which its author aimed. . . . The Christianity which thinks more of soundness of belief than soundness of character is the meanest sort of Christianity, and belongs to an old and outgrown time."

What gave Dr. Holland his unique power to really move men and influence their lives, so that all over the land to-day there are men who are in the thick of the fight of life who say, "I owe that man a great debt," "His words changed my views of life," "He saved me from making a great mistake," "I do not know where I should have landed but for him," and the like? First, it was his peculiar literary style, which was attractive to great numbers of people; the same truths that he enunciated if put into different words, in a different way, would have made no such impression. The analysis of a literary style is like attempting to describe the pleasure of gazing on a beautiful face; you feel the charm, but it is too elusive to be put into words. Critics may wrangle eternally about this redundancy and that deficiency, about how much better it would have been to express the idea in their way, and what a wreck and failure the writer has made of it all; but if he is endowed with the divine gift of uttering truths in a way that interests and pleases his public, he can afford to let the critics keep on wrangling, and hold serenely on his way, sure that he will be loved and remembered after the public has ceased to recall that the critic ever lived.

CHAPTER IX.

The Elements of Dr. Holland's Power—His Religious Experience—Account of Judge Underhill—Spiritual Experience at Richmond—Church Work at Springfield.

IF asked to coin a title for Dr. Holland in reference to the work God had laid out for him, it would read, "The Great Apostle to the Multitudes of Intelligent Americans who have Missed a College Education." There was not the least flavor of bookishness in his writings, they were utterly devoid of the odor of the midnight lamp, yet President Porter, of Yale, said, "He always made a facile use of idiomatic and pure English," and Dr. Bevan, his accomplished New York pastor, said : "In plain nervous speech, with a directness and strength of diction which has few equals among the current writers of the age, he rebuked excesses and abuses of every kind." On the Fourth of July, in the year of Daniel Webster's graduation, he delivered a patriotic address in Hanover, N. H., full of the longest and most sonorous words that his classical synonym-book could supply; of it he afterward said "it was utterly highfalutin." Soon after, he went to Portsmouth to hear Jeremiah Mason endeavor to convince a jury of twelve New Hampshire farmers, in a difficult and complicated case. Said he, "I saw at once that if I was to get my living by convincing such juries I must change my style," and he did, and his speeches are full of those short, Saxon, forceful words, that look simple and innocent but can deal blows like a hammer.

Our Saviour chose fishermen of Galilee to win to him the unlettered masses of his time, who probably had no knowledge whatever of books—probably not even of the three Rs.—and it really was a positive advantage for the work he had to do that Dr. Holland was debarred from obtaining an "Education," so called, with the big E, in his day. His readers didn't suddenly run across references to books or classical allusions which took it for granted that they were familiar with vast provinces of learning, the existence of which is here first unveiled to them, and which produce a sense of missed opportunity and discouragement that to be appreciated needs to be felt. Although Dr. Holland had read the English poets with just discrimination, a true instinct kept him from quoting them, and from interlarding his work with foreign phrases and words—he followed the maxim, "*Look into thine own heart and write.*"

Ten years before he went to Europe President

HIS NEW ENGLANDISM 101

Porter had urged him to go abroad and reside, to study and observe and enlarge his knowledge of men and his ideas. He had answered that he was afraid he should lose the hold he had upon what he deemed his strength, viz., his New England blood, and his familiarity with the convictions and manners and faith of his own people. These he regarded as his capital. Here he felt that he was strong, and he "did not care to relax the energy of these convictions, nor the tenacity of these associations." He knew the secret of the power that had won him his thousands of readers not only in New England, but wherever their lineal successors are found throughout the broad land. But where had he won that wealth of Christian wisdom and spiritual insight and serene conviction that so unerringly guided him to the right side of moral questions, and that gave him the ability to help and comfort so many doubting and inquiring souls? It had been bought with a price, in deep spiritual conflict and suffering.

And how came he by so many of the ideas that were called "advanced" forty years ago, but to-day are accepted as established truths? Where did he learn to sift out the kernel of truth and cast aside the hindering envelope that had shut it in, and kept it from springing up into its natural and symmetrical growth and fruitage?

It is the fashion to call this a day of unbelievers and infidels, but was there ever a time when so many earnest men and women were asking "What is the truth," and saying "Who will show us *the* way?"

Dr. Holland had fought over the whole ground of religious doubt, inch by inch, and had arrived at certain conclusions that for him were inevitable, and at last had had a deep and true religious experience.

Of course he was the possessor of a priceless inheritance in his early education, and in the example of the power of religion to sustain the soul under adversity and disaster, in the life of his father, whose picture he so graphically sketched in the ballad of "Old Daniel Gray." The nature of the causes of the poverty that was his early lot are hinted at in the sketch of Paul Benedict, the inventor, in "Sevenoaks."

Between the years 1836 and 1840 there were a number of "old-fashioned" revivals up and down the Connecticut Valley, and Northampton came in for her share of what was called "seasons of refreshment." Any one who is interested to know how these were "worked up," frequently by people who believed they were doing God's service thereby, will find a highly sympathetic picture of them and their effects in "Arthur Bonnicastle;" into which it is understood there is woven much of the personal experience of the author. Certainly there was much that was factitious and artificial about their inception and conduct, especially as promoted by "evangelists" brought in to assist regular pastors from outside.

To Dr. Holland, with his sensitive imaginative nature, such a season of gloom and terror, and sense of the impending wrath of an offended God, as was the general accompaniment of what was known as a pentecostal season, must have been truly frightful. It is no wonder that calmer, saner people deprecated them, both for their present effects and for the spiritual deadness that was sure to ensue in the inevitable reaction that followed the unnatural excitement. At that day no Christian mother could rest till her children were *in the church;* it was called the "ark of safety," and many entered it, giving assent to creeds that in their youth and inexperience they thought they believed, but to which they had brought no critical analysis, and which were quite sure to haunt them with unanswered and unanswerable questions when their logical faculties should become more developed.

Long before Dr. Holland was twenty-one he had united with a church, the preliminary to which had been assenting to a long and extremely Calvinistic creed, which very likely was the irritant that roused his mind to searching questionings when in the cold light of calm reason he had time to think. It is astonishing to see what heights and depths of unwarranted mystic meaning had been wrought into Christ's simple "This do in remembrance of me." Many joined churches under the impulse of revivals who afterward suffered tortures when the excitement had died out, lest in partaking of the sacrament they were "eating and drinking unworthily," and a person of vivid imagination could easily fancy himself "eating and drinking damnation." They did not perceive that sainthood and sanctification are matters of growth and time, and nearly every town had its man or woman of whom people said in solemn and significant whispers, "Mr. or Mrs. —— doesn't go to the communion now," and it was understood to mean either that there had been a terrible backsliding or that the person was verging on insanity, and as to the numbers who imagined they had committed the unpardonable sin, the record is too distressing: even saintly and devoted pastors sometimes doubted if they had "a right to partake of those blessed seals." If it is asked how could people entertain such extreme and unwarranted notions, it must be answered that they did not accept the New Testament in its simplicity and directness, but tried to believe in systems of man-invented theology founded on it. A very shrewd observer, not of Yankee origin, has said that New England people could not discriminate between what is really in the Bible and what Milton's "Paradise Lost" has made them imagine was in it. Certainly much that was extraneous had been added to the original conception of Christ's beautiful memorial service before it had been endowed with the power to blast the peace and happiness and blight the lives of really saintly men and women, and drive them into insane asylums.

Having attained his majority, Dr. Holland entered the office of Drs. Barrett and Thompson, and his youthful dream of becoming educated was coming true. In the midst of his happiness he had an illustration of the occasional futility of the healing art, and a confirmation of the old tombstone couplet,

> "Friends and physicians could not save
> This mortal body from the grave;"

for no treatment seemed to rescue his favorite sister from the fatal measles, nor the other two from consumption, and henceforth no amount of Christian resignation could obliterate the sorrow that enshrouded the soul of the affectionate mother.

This accumulation of distresses almost frenzied him. He used to walk the streets at night feeling that "God had forgotten the world"—certainly he was hidden from this poor, tempest-tossed creature, who could see no lights coming through rifts in his beclouded sky.

Judge Henry B. Underhill, of California, who knew him intimately at this "storm and stress" period of his life, has kindly prepared a statement as follows:

"I became acquainted with Josiah Gilbert Holland at Northampton, Mass., in the early part of 1840. He was then a medical student in the office of Drs. Barrett and Thompson while I was preparing for college. We sat at the same table and spent much of our leisure time together. The subject of religion was often the topic of our discourse, as we were both church members. His opinions seemed to me unsettled and erratic. He was disposed to question the inspiration of the Scriptures. I recollect that on one occasion he said that we could not depend upon the gospels as recording the words of Christ, for it would be impossible for the disciples who were his companions during the three years of his ministry to remember any considerable portions of what they recorded as the wonderful words that fell from his lips. In reply, I called his attention to the promise of Christ as recorded in the 26th verse of the fourteenth chapter of John's gospel, that the Father would send the Holy Ghost, who would bring all things to their remembrance whatsoever he had said unto them. To my surprise he said that he had never noticed that passage before, but he acknowledged that it was a complete answer to his objection.

He was captious about the efficacy of prayer and other features of practical Christianity, and the impression grew upon me, notwithstanding my admiration and love for him, that he was not a converted man.

"We kept up a correspondence after I left Northampton for Amherst, and he went to Pittsfield to attend medical lectures, and subsequently during his residence as a physician in Springfield, and afterward while he was filling a chair in a commercial college in Richmond, Va. At a certain period during his residence in Richmond he surprised me with a letter which filled my heart with joy. It was like one of the exultant psalms of David. It was an exuberant description of the spiritual illumination which he had experienced. I regret very much that I did not preserve that letter. The love of God and peace in the Lord Jesus, through the abiding presence of the Holy Spirit in his heart, ran through every line. He was then a humble child at the foot of the cross. No more doubts about the inspiration of the Scriptures, no more cavilling concerning the plan of salvation through the Divine Redeemer. All the essentials were plain to him.

"I met him afterward in Mississippi, then at Springfield, where he was the Superintendent of the Sabbath-school, then in New York, and though many years had intervened, and the results of a busy life-work were before the world in the products of his pen, his simple faith in Christ was still the conspicuous feature of his character. He was a *practical* Christian, laying little or no stress upon the theories of the theologians, but zealous for the development of the Christian graces, which are catalogued in the first chapter of the Second Epistle of Peter."

It was seven years from the time when Mr. Underhill's record of the student-communings begins, to what may be called that spiritual culmination in Richmond. During the early part of the time Dr. Holland had reached one goal of his ambition in gaining his medical diploma. He had married a deeply religious woman, though one who had a wholly different type of mind from his; he had made the unsuccessful experiments in a profession for which he had no true vocation, and being unsuccessful had passed through a most unpleasant worldly "valley of humiliation," and now, at last, had emerged into God's own light, and had yielded a complete and ungrudging allegiance to the Lord Jesus Christ—to use his own words, to "the personal representative of Jehovah on earth." Some of these wrestlings with himself, when the way seemed dark before him, Bunyan would have called "the buffetings of Satan," but they may be characterized as the questionings of an awakened soul before some of the deep mysteries of life and Providence. Graphic descriptions of them have found place in the pages of "Kathrina," a book that will have readers till the New England Puritan mind is sophisticated into something quite different from itself. When he came back from Richmond he at once established family prayers, and those who had the privilege of uniting with them, saw what a sincere act of worship he made them, that they were his " soul's sincere desire, uttered ; " they learned what a living and unfaltering faith Dr. Holland had that the God he believed in had the power to impart right impulses to the wavering and uncertain human soul halting between two courses of action, and that in the day of trouble there is but one sure way that leads out into the light beyond it—to pray. In looking back upon those early days of doubt and questionings, from a time very near the end of his life, he confided to Dr. Bevan that he had gone through them with a sad heart ; and people who flippantly toss off the epithets " infidel," " unbeliever," " disorganizer," when a man cannot take his religion cut and dried at second hands, and speak as if the inquiring mind was guilty of wilful defiance of God's law, might sometimes better spare their crude misjudgments.

It was very evident from Dr. Holland's after-history, that during those years of incertitude he had thought deeply not only on his own personal experiences, but on religious questions generally, and meanwhile he strove to use his powers and exert his influence for the building up of God's kingdom, whether at peace in his own mind or not, and the clear convictions that he arrived at eventually, seem to furnish an instance of the fulfilment of the promise that the man who will "do" God's will shall "know" of his doctrine. In a certain measure he blazed out a new path, and consequently was for many years more or less misunderstood by people whose good opinion he would have liked, could it have been purchased without a sacrifice of his convictions.

He connected himself with the South Church in Springfield soon after his marriage, when Rev. Noah Porter, afterward President at Yale, was the pastor, and an attachment grew up between them that only ended with Dr. Holland's life. Here he had a Bible class of young men, and in teaching them expressed what were then called "liberal" views, the adjective generally being construed to mean latitudinarian, and he had already caught some glimpses of that latter-day reformation in religious teaching that was going to replace assent to a series of theological dogmas by active religious life. He probably made the class interesting. At all events it soon got abroad that he was teaching "heresy," and a meeting of deacons *et al.* was called to look into the matter and remonstrate. A very small minority only disapproved, and his answer was to read a chapter in the New Testament saying, "That is my creed, and I must teach the Scriptures as they seem to me; Christ's theology is the material for me." He had also intimated that the class need not pay too much heed to the Old Testament. A recent preacher has said: "The conservative forces of institutional religion have never been able to welcome new truth, or new methods of teaching truth; always the worshippers of the past have resisted the innovations, as heresies, of the workers for the future." At that date to hold unorthodox views was to forfeit social caste, and a different type of man would have kept quiet; but Dr. Holland was too true to his convictions to be capable of such a time-serving policy; but he gave up his class, to their loss no doubt. Rev. Mr. Buckingham afterward became the pastor of the church, and in a memorial address said: "He followed the dictates of his heart rather than the teachings of any theological school, and drinking in the spirit of Christ he never was guilty of heresy; he adored and trusted in Jesus Christ as the only Saviour of men, and he was always true to such a Christianity, whether in his Sunday-school teachings, or the daily newspaper, or monthly periodical, or in his novels and poems."

CHAPTER X.

Church Connections—Dr. Gladden's Memorial Sermon—Influence of Dr. Drummond—Formation of the Memorial Church—Association with the "Brick Church"—Teaching Sunday School in Paris—Conversation with Mr. De Vries—"Arthur Bonnicastle."

It was while he was absent in the South that he had passed through the remarkable illuminating spiritual experience described by Mr. Underhill, and he undoubtedly felt more deeply than ever the obligation to let his light shine. After consultation with Dr. Buckingham he decided to unite with the North Church, then young and growing—keeping step with the rapid growth of Springfield itself. He said it was a church that he could help, and, says Dr. Buckingham, "In addition to his faithful work here in the social and religious life of the church, he made himself especially valuable as the leader of the choir. You should have seen him sing as well as heard him, to understand what he meant by the service of song in the house of the Lord! His noble mien, his reverent and exultant manner as he carried the praises of the congregation up to heaven! The picture of the choir-boys is a pleasant one, but commonplace in comparison with this magnificent specimen of manhood and Christian service." Dr. Gladden, after alluding to a very busy period in his life, in a memorial sermon, in speaking of his singing, said: "During all this time he was also the leader of the choir. I shall always remember him as I heard his pure tenor voice in the gallery of the North Church in 1859. He stood there with his hymn-book level with his eyes singing, 'Jesus, lover of my soul,' to a beautiful selection. It was quite evident to one who saw and heard him singing that it was something more than a performance, it was worship. His services in connection with this choir, his faithfulness in making long journeys, when on his lecturing tours, to be at his post every Sunday, have been referred to in the journals, and the circumstance was characteristic of the man. It should also be noted that this was wholly a labor of love on his part; the parish made an appropriation for music, but he took none of it; what he did was done heartily, as unto the Lord."

Of course, with his sensitive musical ear and his fine voice he loved the work; but he was no less faithful in the laborious, difficult, and often thankless position of Parish Committeeman, and when he resigned, in July, 1856, to go with a colony to form a new church in a still newer field, the parish showed that they appreciated these faithful self-sacrificing services by a cordial vote of thanks.

During his connection with that church it had fallen to his lot to aid in the selection of a pastor, and the one that his choice fell on was a rarely gifted man, and there was something in him that bound him most sympathetically to the heart of Dr. Holland. Dr. Gladden, who knew Dr. Holland very intimately, thus speaks of him and of them. In a memorial sermon, preached in the North Church, where Dr. Holland had been a living force for twelve years, he said: "In studying the influences that helped to shape his character, I think we shall be led to put much emphasis on the ministrations of this true servant of God. Mr. Drummond was a minister quite out of the common. He was a seer, a poet, a teacher of lofty inspiration, a liberal man in the best sense of that word. Brave, open-minded, full of enthusiasm, the sermons that he has left show what manner of man he was. Dr. Holland had always been a good writer, skilful and happy in his way of putting things; but it was not until Mr. Drummond became his pastor and friend that his writings began to assume that lofty quality, that prophetic tone which was the secret of his power. The 'Titcomb Letters' were written in 1858. Mr. Drummond's pastorate began in June of that year. Of course this element was in the man, but I am sure that the fire of Mr. Drummond's inspired enthusiasm helped to bring it out; and I shall always believe that through this short ministry of James Drummond a great moral quickening was given to Dr. Holland, and through him to the world." What Dr. Holland's own opinion of moral quickenings was, and of their incontestable power, will be seen later on.

Dr. Holland felt that many more men than are, should be in the church; he studied and thought much over the problem why so many men whose "walk and conversation" are pure and upright, and who certainly are not indifferent to the claims of Christ, are still not members of His church. He felt that a man's power for good was greatly enhanced by his being visibly enrolled as a soldier of the cross; he had little sympathy with the notion that "a good man can do just as much good out of the church as in it," and he knew that many men who would willingly own Christ as the guide of their lives were deterred from publicly uniting with any church through inability to give their assent to certain statements in old creeds, which, however much of vital truth they may have held for the men who first formulated them, have long since lost their significance for the men of to-day. He also felt that non-essential forms of worship built up needless barriers to Christian communion among men who give a hearty and unreserved assent to the claims of Christ on them for active service, and he thought he saw a field of usefulness for an evangelical but undenominational church in Ward I. of Springfield. An active sympathizer and coadjutor with Dr. Holland in this project was Mr. George M. Atwater, and fifty-five members of the North Church, under the leadership of these two, went forth and formed the Memorial Church—its name being a recognition of what they knew had been the sincere and consecrated and godly labors of the *deceased ministers of New England.*

A silver plate containing what may be called the "platform" of this church bore this inscription:

"From love to God and good-will to man, a company of believers who profess faith in Christ, the Saviour of mankind, by the aid of the churches of Springfield, and other friends of the enterprise, build this house of worship for the Memorial Church. This church, constituted by the fellowship of Christians of different denominations, was organized October 29, 1865, and named the Memorial Church in memory of the deceased ministers of New England.

"Other foundation can no man lay than that is laid, which is Jesus Christ.—1 Cor. iii. 11.

"The Lord our God be with us, as he was with our fathers: let him not leave us, nor forsake us:

"That he may incline our hearts unto him, to walk in all his ways, and to keep his commandments, and his statutes, and his judgments, which he commanded our fathers.—1 Kings viii. 57, 58."

Such a radically new departure as this was, thirty years ago, was bound to encounter opposition, and Dr. Buckingham in his address at the memorial meeting said: "He found no sympathy, I am ashamed to say, among some of our church members and ministers, for obstacles were placed in his way and he was needlessly perplexed; and if he had not loved the cause of Christ more than most, he never would have sacrificed his peace of mind and continued to push on to success as he did this enterprise. He once said to me: 'Christianity, in the form of abstract statement, and in the shape of a creed, has not for me any particular interest nor very much meaning; I have to test things through my heart and best feelings. If they seem good and true and like Christ, it satisfies me, and nothing else does.'"

At the end of a year the church passed some "resolutions" which show how well the plan had worked, and as a specimen of a church organized with apostolic simplicity they are here reproduced. Their preamble says:

"Believing that an organized company of believers in Jesus Christ, and who acknowledge him to be the Saviour of mankind, form and constitute a

Christian church; that a Congregational church is one which vests all ecclesiastical power in a company thus organized, and that the Holy Catholic Church is the universal Christian brotherhood; therefore,

"1. Resolved, That the Memorial Church of Springfield, having declared in its creed its belief in the Holy Catholic Church, welcomes to its membership and communion all who love the Lord Jesus Christ in sincerity and truth, and who agree with it concerning the essential doctrines of the Christian religion, by whatever name they may be called.

"2. That the success of the church upon this basis during the first year of its history—a success which has brought at least five denominations into a happy communion of personal feeling and action—is our sufficient justification for reaffirming this basis as a ground of Christian liberality, a guide to a wise and sound policy, and especially as the true basis for organized Christian effort in the ward in which our church is located."

All this has been put in practice in so many places now, that it seems commonplace, if not trite and stale; but thirty years ago it was a discovery. The church retained much in its formal confession of faith that would be eliminated to-day as extraneous and unnecessary, but, these innovators had to throw a sop to the over-tender theological conscience of the day. At the end of the third year of its life Dr. Holland went to Europe, and soon after removed to

New York, but the church thrived, and a recent programme of its services and activities, for a single week, shows that it is a live church, and doing a work that reaches old and middle-aged and young.

On removing to New York Dr. Holland allied himself to what is known as the Brick Church, and at once responded to all calls upon him in church or parish work.

During all his life he was an active participator in Sunday-school work, either as teacher or superintendent, and even when "recreating" in Paris took charge of the Sunday-school in the American Church there. Wherever he went he did not allow himself to become an idler in the Master's vineyard.

A few short extracts from his "Topics of the Time" will show how thoroughly he comprehended that transformation in the depraved which we call repentance: "The greatness of the founder of Christianity is conspicuously shown in his passing by social institutions as of minor and inconsiderable importance and fastening his claims upon the individual. The reform of personal character was his one aim, with him the man was great, and the institution small. There was but one way with him for making a good society, and that was by the purification of its individual materials. There can be nothing more radical than this; and there never was anything—there never will be anything—to take the place of it. . . ."

"It is most interesting and instructive, we repeat, to observe how all the patent methods that have been adopted outside of, or in opposition to, Christianity, for the reformation of society, have, one after the other, gone to the wall, or gone to the dogs. A dream and a few futile or disastrous experiments are all that ever comes of them. Societies, communities, organizations melt away and are lost, and all that remains of them is their history. We suppose it is a wonder to such men that Mr. Moody and Mr. Sankey can obtain such a following as they do. They undoubtedly attribute it to superstition and ignorance, but these reformers are simply eminent radicals after the Christian pattern, who deal with the motives and means furnished them by the one great radical reformer of the world—Jesus Christ himself. . . . No good society can possibly be made out of bad materials, and when the materials are made good the society takes a good form naturally, as a pure salt makes its crystal without superintendence. Christian reform, with all its motives and methods, is found to be just as vital to-day as it ever was. It is the same yesterday, to-day, and forever. . . . As near as we can ascertain, Mr. Moody has not paid very much attention to the preaching of Judaism—involving a theism and a system of doctrine which Christ came to set aside and supersede. Paul resolved that he wouldn't know anything but Jesus Christ, and we are inclined to think that Mr. Moody doesn't know anything but Jesus Christ. . . . Our preachers, as a rule, know so many things besides the Master; they have wrought up such a complicated scheme, based upon a thousand other things than Jesus Christ, that they confess they don't understand it themselves, and yet we are assured that the path of life is so plain that a wayfaring man though a fool need not err therein. And considering the fact that Christ is in himself *the* Way, *the* Truth, and *the* Life, and considering also the use that has been made of the Bible in complicating and loading down his simple religion with the theological inventions of men, it may legitimately be questioned whether the progress of Christianity has not been hindered by our possession of all the sacred books outside of the evangelical histories."

"The simple vital truth as it is in Jesus Christ, and not as it is in Moses or Daniel or Jeremiah, or anybody else, for that matter, is what the world wants." Dr. Holland would have echoed the sentiment of the Rev. Dr. Taylor, of the Broadway Tabernacle, that it was a mercy no more of all Christ's sayings and doings were recorded; for, said he, "a book that costs five cents, and can be carried in the vest-pocket, contains all the essentials of salvation."

Of the beautiful summer home, Bonnie-Castle, at Alexandria Bay, there have been descriptions and pictures; but when Dr. Holland betook himself thither for his summer rest he did not leave his religion behind. He at once interested himself in the welfare of the little "Reformed" church there, contributing generously to its funds, and sustaining its ordinances with his presence, and its pastor with his love and confidence.

In earnest conversations with the Rev. Mr. De Vries, its pastor, he told the story of his early spiritual struggles, and it may light some tempest-tossed soul over a dark and stormy way. It is certain that could he know that, he would consent to its repetition here. He said to that excellent man, "When little more than a boy, I felt it my duty to join the church, and did. I had many doubts and struggles, sometimes behaved in a manner not becoming a member of the church; yet at communion seasons I felt it my right and duty to partake of the sacrament, though many seemed to think I had no right whatever. So I clung to the church. At twenty-eight years of age I left my home in Springfield for the South, leaving my young wife behind, because necessity compelled me. In my adversity an inexpressible sadness came over me. I wept

and prayed, day and night, in the school and in the fields; prayed as I never prayed before—prayer which God heard, for then His peace came upon me." Mr. De Vries says, "That was the simple story of his conversion."

But what of the seven long intervening years? Did he ever become indifferent to his duty as far as he saw it? Did he starve his soul, as thousands of our young men do, and remain away from church, because he could not yield an intellectual assent to all the dogmas contained in the creeds? No, he still continued to seek, faithfully performing the duty that lay next to his hand—strove to make himself a useful and valuable man in medicine, and when he found himself unadapted to it, he still strove to provide things honest in the sight of all men for himself and his, and while in the faithful performance of this first and nearest duty of all men, God's light shone into his soul, as it certainly would not have done had he ceased to strive to enter in at the strait gate. During those seven years of conflict and unrest he "thought and thought and thought," on the vital problems of religion—the soul's relation to God in all the varied phases of life. He wrought out for himself a clear solution of many of the most perplexing problems which he was to elucidate to many other inquiring minds, when he should realize that the materials in which he was set to work were the most impalpable of all things, but when moulded by their own heaven-appointed artificers, will outlast empires. Of these "words" he says: "When the artist works with these he works with that by which God made the universe; and there is no genuine embodiment of the highest life of man which passes so directly into the life of other men as that which takes the form of words. The pencil and the chisel are but clumsy things by the side of the pen—the choicest and noblest of all instruments ever placed in human fingers."

With this recital as the "key," we read between the lines in "Arthur Bonnicastle." He has been speaking of the restraining force that the mere fact of his being a church-member had exercised over him, though he had violated his conscience in many ways in those young days, and says: "But this was not all. My life had come into the line of the divine plan for my own Christian development. I had been a recipient all my life; now I had become an active power. I had all my life been appropriating the food that came to me, and amusing myself with the playthings of fancy and imagination; now I had begun to act, and expend in earnest work for worthy objects. The spiritual attitude effected by this change was one which brought me face to face with all that was unworthy in me and in my past life, and I felt myself under the influence of a mighty regenerating power, which I had no disposition to resist. I could not tell whence it came nor whither it went. . . . There was no outcry, no horror of great darkness, no disposition to publish, but a subtle, silent, sweet revolution. As it went on within me, I grew stronger day by day, and my life and work were flooded with the light of a great and fine significance. Sensibility softened, and endurance hardened under it."

His own explanation of this "psychological experience" follows in the next paragraph: "Spirit of God, thou didst not thunder on Sinai amidst the smoke and tempest; but in the burning bush thou didst appear in a flame that warmed without withering, and illuminated without consuming. Thou didst not hang upon the cross on Calvary, but thou didst stir the hearts of the bereaved disciples as they walked in the way with their risen Lord. . . . Was this conversion? It was not an intellectual matter at all. I had changed no opinions, for the unworthy opinions I had acquired had fallen from me, one by one, as my practice had conformed more and more to the Christian standard. . . . My deepest intellectual convictions remained precisely what they had always been. No, it was a spiritual quickening. It had been winter with me, and I had been covered with snow and locked with ice. Did I melt the bonds which held me, by warmth self-generated? Does the rose do this, or the violet? There was a sun in some heaven I could not see that shone upon me. There was a wind from some far latitude that breathed upon me. To be quickened is to be touched by a vital finger. To be quickened is to receive a fructifying flood from the great source of light."

He makes his hero refer to two spiritual crises in his life, but says neither change was conversion, and then gives this theory: "Far back in childhood, at my mother's knee, at my father's side, and in my own secret chamber, those changes were wrought which had directed my life toward a Christian consummation. My little rivulet was flowing toward the sea, increasing as it went, when it was disturbed by the first awful experiences of my life; and its turbid waters were never, until this later time, wholly clarified. . . . If my later experience was conversion, then conversion may come to a man every year of his life. It was simply a revivification and reinforcement of the powers and processes of spiritual life. It was ministry direct and immediate, to development and growth; and with me it was complete restoration to the track of my Christian boyhood. . . . I learned then, what the world is slow to learn, that there can be no true happiness that is not the result of the action of harmonious powers steadily bent upon pursuits that seek a worthy end, and that it can never be grasped and held save by true manhood and womanhood." Are we to infer that no temptations ever came to him, that the final victory was won in this hour of "clear shining after rain?" Far from it. The conquest of grace over a naturally sensitive temper and a proud spirit was not won without effort. He once confessed, in a very intimate conversation, "I must acknowledge every day that I find every sin, at least the germ of every sin, in my own heart." From the day of this great quickening he was God's willing servant, ever working as if in the Master's eye, and with his face steadily set toward the Heavenly City, and very likely was sustained and comforted on the way by the ministrations of such a spiritually gifted man as the Rev. Mr. Drummond. Certain it is he learned that he had the gift of touching the hearts and influencing the lives of the great masses of the plain people, and long before he died millions of them had had their lives touched to finer issues by those *words* among which was not one that needed to be repented of in the great hour of his own final judgment.

CHAPTER XL

Literary Success a Plant of Slow Growth—"Bitter-Sweet" published when he was Forty—Criticisms of It—James Russell Lowell's review in *The Atlantic Monthly* — "Thanksgiving Day"—Observations on the Bible.

FEW literary men have seemed to have such a definite conception of the place they were fitted for and were resolved to fill as Browning. From the time when he began to think at all on a life-work he was resolved *to be a poet*. His circumstances left him free of care for livelihood, and there was no danger that his physical wants would fail of being supplied even if his books did not sell. When Dr. Holland was but a youth, *to be a poet*, seemed to him the loftiest and most desirable of human destinies, and he never could recall the time when the dream of being one did not haunt his thoughts. When we recall the fact that many of the finest poets have had to wait through long years for recognition, and that this man was compelled to take his place among those of the world's workers who could produce something adapted to immediate intellectual consumption, we do not wonder that his first distinctive "Poem" made its appearance when he was forty years old—"Bitter-Sweet" was published in 1859. It took a dramatic form, and into it are distilled Dr. Holland's reflections on the mysteries of Life and Death, on the soul-wracking problems of Doubt and Faith, on the existence of Evil as one of the vital conditions of the universe, on the questions of Predestination, Original Sin, Free-will, and the whole haunting brood of Calvinistic theological metaphysics, these last being what Emerson calls the "mumps and measles of the soul"—they may not kill, but are full of discomfort while being endured. In the next century people will refer to it, to learn exactly what a New England Thanksgiving was like, while it yet remained the crowning festival of the year, for a people who were unsophisticated by travel and communication with others whose high yearly festival was Christmas. But under and through all disguises of rhyme and rhythm, of blank verse and careful scansion, of question, rejoinder, and song, there is ever seen the face and form of the ineradicable preacher. Old Froissart says "the English take their pleasures seriously," and in "Bitter-Sweet," where some passages are attempted in what we call the "lighter vein," it is perfectly plain that Dr. Holland, who was "English," and a great deal more, could never trifle successfully.

All those writers who have really touched the

hearts of men have looked within themselves and transcribed what they have found there before they could win a sympathetic hearing. Emerson says: "Every man's condition is a solution in hieroglyphic to those inquiries he would put. He acts it as life before he apprehends it as truth." In a discussion on the uses of Evil, in "Bitter-Sweet" David says to Ruth,

> "Thus to me
> Evil is not a mystery, but a means
> Selected from the infinite resource
> To make the most of me."

His interlocutor—Ruth—begins to be convinced and to recall examples; and says:

> "I see a youth whom God has crowned with power,
> And cursed with poverty. With bravest heart
> He struggles with his lot, through toilsome years,—
> Kept to his task by daily want of bread,
> And kept to virtue by his daily task,—
> Till, gaining manhood in the manly strife,—
> The fire that fills him smitten from a flint—
> The strength that arms him wrested from a fiend—
> He stands, at last, a master of himself,
> And, in that grace, a master of his kind."

No prima donna thinks she has exhibited all her powers till she has essayed a "Cradle Song" for us, and all of the great poets have attempted to record their speculations anent infancy in literature, but few of them have ever achieved a cleverer bit of genuine "baby-talk" than is to be found in the passage where Ruth bends over the cradle and lulls her young nephew to sleep with a rhythmical mixture of nonsense and philosophy about those

> "Barks that were launched on the other side,
> And slipped from Heaven on an ebbing tide."

Many of the opinions that had crystallized in his mind have become commonplace to-day—they found a voice in this poem. He knew that there are hours in the brightest lives when the stars seem to have gone out, and the soul feeling itself in the grasp of forces which it can neither defy nor conquer, can only moan out its misery. In a "Song of Doubt," we hear their wail :

> " The day is quenched, and the sun is fled ;
> God has forgotten the world!
> The moon is gone, and the stars are dead ;
> God has forgotten the world !
>
> " Evil has won in the horrid feud
> Of ages with The Throne ;
> Evil stands on the neck of Good,
> And rules the world alone.
> . . . . . .
>
> " What are prayers in the lips of death,
> Filling and chilling with hail ?
> What are prayers but wasted breath,
> Beaten back by the gale.'"

And in the "Song of Faith" he voices the spirit of the hours when the soul is flooded with ineffable joy, and is convinced that

> "Day will return with a fresher boon ;
> God will remember the world!
> Night will come with a newer moon ;
> God will remember the world!"

> "Evil is only slave of Good,
> Sorrow the servant of Joy ;"
> . . . . . .

> "The fountain of joy is fed by tears,
> And love is lit by the breath of sighs,
> The deepest griefs and the wildest fears
> Have holiest ministries."

He had pondered the mysteries of Pain and Death,

> "Life evermore is fed by death,
> In earth and sea and sky ;
> And, that a rose may breathe its breath,
> Something must die.

> "Earth is a sepulchre of flowers,
> Whose vitalizing mould
> Through boundless transmutation towers,
> In green and gold.
> . . . . . .

> "The falcon preys upon the finch,
> The finch upon the fly,
> And nought will loose the hunger-pinch
> But death's wild cry.
> . . . . . .

> "From lowly woe springs lordly joy ;
> From humble good diviner ;
> The greater life must aye destroy
> And drink the minor.
>
> "From hand to hand life's cup is passed
> Up Being's piled gradation,
> Till men to angels yield at last
> The rich collation."

And really the burden of the poem is to show God's uses for evil, in fitting his principal character through suffering, for "saintship in Christ—the Manhood Absolute!"

Nothing in life so resembles putting a window over the heart as for an "earnest man" to bring out a poem into which he has condensed so much of his own experience and thought as make it truly his. He listens with trembling anxiety for those echoes that shall assure him whether in the poet's pre-eminent office of *seer* he has discovered anything not found before, whether he had anything new to tell, or if he has been able to set old truths at new angles, so that they could send scintillant and penetrating rays into hitherto unillumined corners. Dr. Holland had his full share of this expectant sensitiveness, and so we can imagine how the critique of the *Atlantic Monthly*—then, more than now, the recognized arbiter of literary fate—was looked for ; but only a writer can appreciate such praise as this : "'Bitter-

Sweet' is truly an original poem—as genuine a product of our soil as a golden-rod or an aster. It is as purely American—nay, more than that, as purely New English, as the poems of Burns or Scott were Scotch. We read ourselves gradually back to our boyhood in it, and were aware of a flavor in it deliciously local and familiar—a kind of sour-sweet, as in a *frozen*-thaw apple. From the title to the last line it is delightfully characteristic. The family-party met for Thanksgiving can hit on no better way to be jolly than in a discussion of the Origin of Evil, and the Yankee husband (a shooting-star in the quiet haven of village morals) about to run away from his wife can be content with no less comet-like vehicle than a balloon. The poem is Yankee, even to the questionable extent of substituting 'locality' for 'scene' in the stage directions; and we feel sure that none of the characters ever went to bed in their lives, but always sidled through the more decorous subterfuge of 'retiring.'

"We could easily show that 'Bitter-Sweet' was not this and that and t'other, but, after all said and done, it would remain an obstinately charming little book. It is not free from faults of taste, nor from a certain commonplaceness of metre; but Mr. Holland always saves himself in some expression so simply poetical, some image so fresh and natural, the harvest of his own heart and eye, that we are ready to forgive him all faults in our thankfulness at finding the soul of Theocritus transmigrated into the body of a Yankee.

"It would seem the simplest thing in the world to be able to help yourself to what lies all around you ready to your hand; but writers of verse commonly find it a difficult, if not impossible, thing to do. Conscious that a certain remoteness from ordinary life is essential in poetry, they aim at it by laying their scenes far away in time, and taking their images from far away in space—thus contriving to be foreign at once to their century and their country. Such self-made exiles and aliens are never repatriated by posterity. It is only here and there that a man is found like Hawthorne, Judd, and Mr. Holland, who discovers or instinctively feels that this remoteness is attained and attainable only by lifting up and transfiguring the ordinary and familiar with the *mirage* of the ideal. We mean it as very high praise when we say that 'Bitter-Sweet' is one of the few books that have found the secret of drawing up and assimilating the juices of this New World of ours."

This was the critical and analytical judgment of no less a man than James Russell Lowell—and with the sweet consciousness that *he* approved it, Dr. Holland could afford to let lesser men carp at and ridicule it, and whether you agree or dissent, when you go to his publisher's ledger you will learn that more than ninety thousand copies of the book have been sold, and that there is still an ever fresh demand for it, and you will realize that it touched a responsive chord in what is ignorantly judged to be the impassive Yankee breast.

What was the secret of this power, of this spell which he wove over so many of the plain, hardworking people of New England. One example will supply the answer. He wrote, very soon after he became connected with the *Republican*, an editorial on "Thanksgiving Day"—this was many years before the appearance of "Bitter-Sweet." It really is a prose poem of great vividness and beauty, and it was because the spirit of this uniquely local Thanksgiving festival of his region and his time had penetrated his inmost soul, that he could sketch its lineaments, and lift it up into the transfiguring light which remains imperishable, while the festival itself, in its most marked features, is fading away or merging in the more universal one of Christmas.

A native New England publisher—a good judge of literary work—thinks the "Cotter's Saturday Night" itself does not surpass it in its pictures of homely happiness. This may be extravagant praise, but a sentence or two will show how he could use the short, simple, Saxon elements of our language, and the sympathy that could understand the attitude of every class toward it exhibits "the hidings of his power."

"*Once more the Puritan Anniversary!* Wherever the heart of a child of New England beats to-day, it warms in the fire of tender memories, and throbs to the touch of happy or sad associations. From Western forests, from Southern everglades, from the golden gulches and treasure-laden river-beds of California, from every country under the whole heaven, and from every sea that mirrors the stars and stripes, the thoughts—the yearning thoughts—of thousands, nay, millions, come teeming home. The fires that glow upon our hearths to-day shine out through all the world. The kiss that rings in the hall, as the dear friends come in—the father, the mother, the sister, the brother—and lay aside their furs and the dusty gear of travel, flies on the wings of the wind, and melts like a snowflake, cooled by distance, but really from heaven, on the trembling lip of fancy, thousands of weary miles away. Present in spirit at our smoking boards to-day are all the rovers. The blithe Thanksgiving bells are heard by listening travellers all over life's weary desert." Then he draws pictures of the festival as kept in the home of wealth; in the laborer's cottage, where the daughter has returned from the factory, bearing gifts to all the younger children; in the poor widow's cottage, who has been endowed with plenteous bounties; in the home of the young couple just setting out on their married life; then of the home where the aged father and mother no longer sit at the board, till all the phases of life have been represented; but we quote only one: "*Pile on the logs!* Let the flame go dancing up the chimney. We are all together once more. The father with his thin hair sits in his easy-chair, and the good old mother is busy about the house. The favorite son and his chosen companion have come home, and merry children bear them company. His manly voice rings through the old house once more, and how much good it does the old man's heart to hear it. The sweet girl who went out with the stranger is at her father's feet as in days long gone by, and the womanly dignity which she has learned to wear, and the independent spirit she has striven to cherish before the world, have given way, and, melted in tears of love and gratitude—she is a blessed child again. Listen to the merry prattle in the room. For twenty years the house has not echoed with such music. And how the stream of talk flows on in happy volubility! This is Thanksgiving in one house." Then at the close the inborn preacher that he was asserted itself thus: "With bended knees, with overflowing hearts, with kindly benevolent emotions, with glad and contented minds, with subdued and penitent spirits, let us make return for all the blessings of the year. Thus shall the future be bathed in a brighter light, and the returning holidays, that stand like golden altars along the pathway of the future, their calm smoke ascending up to heaven, shall make all the road look hallowed and hopeful." The plainest working-man could make those pictures his own.

As there are at least a thousand persons born with the critical faculty to one who has the creative gift, each new literary production has to run the gauntlet of the nine hundred and ninety-nine who couldn't have done the work of the thousandth man, but who can see all its defects and shortcomings, and "Bitter-Sweet" was no exception, and as an animal stung by a wasp, while lying at ease on the green grass of a sunny, breeze-swept pasture, concentrates all its thoughts for the time on the sting, to the exclusion of all the delights of the situation, so an author suffers from what he inevitably considers an unjust estimate of his work. George Eliot showed her wisdom in running away to the Continent every time she put forth a new book, for even her consummate gifts couldn't abash the critics. As the great sale of the book had not yet attested its genuine qualities, the buzz of the stingers hurt and depressed Dr. Holland, and just at this time a little circumstance occurred that helped to reassure him, and it always lingered in his memory as a bright episode. Among the corps of instructors at the Maplewood Institute of Pittsfield, then a prominent and flourishing school for young women, there chanced to be a man who could write pleasing song-music, and another man truly accomplished in all the "business" pertaining to theatrical representations. Between them they arranged from "Bitter-Sweet" a very clever "dramatic episode," to be acted and sung by the pupils at Christmas. A friend invited Dr. and Mrs. Holland to come to Pittsfield and witness the performance, which was very creditably done, in the presence of an audience consisting of the *élite* of the town, who frequently manifested their approbation. At the close the Rev. John Todd, who had a happy gift for *impromptu* and occasional speeches, made a little address congratulating the author, and the praise was especially grateful to the man, who, as a poor medical student, having brought no letters of introduction to influential people, had passed two rather unsatisfactory lecture-terms in the town, and had felt a little sore over what seemed an undeserved obscurity. Another grateful coincidence was the fact that the Rev. Dr. Todd had been the pastor of the Edwards church in Northampton at the time when Dr. Holland was fighting his poverty by teaching penmanship in his out-of-school time. What was native and genuine in each of two truly original men

sprang to greet its like in the other, and though
often differing in opinion they were the firmest of
friends thereafter, and very long afterward Dr. Holland said to the lady who had secured his presence
at the "play," with ardent expressions of gratitude,
" You took pains to be kind to me when I needed it."

But there was another quite unexpected effect of
the publication of "Bitter-Sweet," which at the present time will hardly be believed, and which cannot
be justly estimated without taking into consideration
the fact that it was published before the volcanic
outburst of the war, when people still had a great
deal of time for the introspective analysis of their
moods and spiritual "states," and were given to
hair-splitting speculations on the "soundness" of
tenets, and many were endowed with both taste and
leisure for marking the slightest deviations from the
beaten paths of orthodoxy—in short, were heresy-hunters, believing themselves largely warranted in
criticising and regulating the "walk and conversation," if not the consciences, of others. These were
generally persons scarcely fitted to enter into the
spirit of an imaginative work; they could not separate the artist from the man, and some of them
seemed to think the author ought to be able to lay
his hand on his heart and make oath to every opinion
and action as a "true fact" of his own belief and experience. From the time when Dr. Holland had

advised his Bible Class to pay more attention to the doctrines and life of Christ, and less to those of Moses and David and Daniel, he had been somewhat of an orthodox suspect, and he felt that by a certain conservative, ultra-respectable class of men —some of them of pure and beautiful private lives and actuated by the loftiest of motives—his sentiments were regarded with disfavor—he thought undeserved disfavor. With them he certainly had lost caste by the publication of views that they rated dangerous and "shaky." He felt himself misunderstood, and it was while he was being made to feel the chill of this unsympathetic atmosphere that the shock came by which all the dreamers and theorizers were rudely shaken from their speculations by the call "to arms," and the man who could crush down all selfish aims, and respond in obedience to the great "*I* OUGHT *to go*," was seen to be the man of true worth, whatever views he may have held on Speculative Theology. During those four years of agony the New England mind underwent a revolution in its standards of judgment upon conduct, and in that great upheaval were laid the foundations of that re-examination, with new illumination, of time-worn beliefs, and that reorganization of creeds, which, as Whittier says, make it "seem as if the foundations are breaking up," and he hopes "that if the planks and stagings of human device give way we shall find the Eternal Rock beneath. . . . We cannot do without God, and of him we are sure." To Dr. Holland, too, it was given never for one moment to miss a living faith in the Fatherhood of God, and in the leadership and Brotherhood of Christ.

Meantime the multitudes of men and women who had read the poem and his other books wanted to see and hear their author, and on the lecture platform he showed the same insight into the popular heart, and the same mastery of the keys that open it, that had commended his books to the multitude. In this series of lectures, studied by the light of thirty years after, it is easy to see how really "original" were the views he held on all the moral and religious questions of the time. As great a hater of shams as Carlyle himself, he took a less startling way of shattering them, and seeing plainly the folly of trying to guide the footsteps of to-day by the light of lamps that went out hundreds of years ago, he did his best to persuade people to drop the lamps and get new ones. His observations on the Bible—on which he had thought and studied much—show him as an *avant-coureur* of the agitation that is to-day disturbing Christendom. "There is a good deal of irrational reverence for the Bible. There are men who carry a Bible with them wherever they go as a sort of protection to them. There are men who read it daily, not because they are truth-seekers, but because they are favor-seekers. To read it is a part of their duty. To neglect to read it would be to court adversity. There are men who open it at random to see what special message God has for them through the ministry of chance or miracle. There are men who hold it as a sort of fetich, and bear it about with them as if it were an idol. There are men who see God in *it*, and see Him nowhere else. The wonderful words printed upon the starry heavens; the music of the ministry that comes to them in winds and waves and in the songs of birds; the multiplied forms of beauty that smile upon them from streams and flowers, and lakes and landscapes; the great scheme of beneficent service by which they receive their daily bread and their clothing and shelter—all these are unobserved, or fail to be recognized as divine. In short, there is to them no expression of God except what they find in a book. And this book is so sacred that even the form of language into which it has been imperfectly translated is sacred. They would not have a word changed. They would recoil from any attempt to examine critically into the sources of the book, forgetting that they are rational beings, and that one of the uses of their rational faculties is to know whereof they affirm, and to give a reason for the faith and hope that are in them."

On creeds, he says: " Old creeds cannot possibly contain the present life and thought and opinion, old ideas whose vitality has long been expended—there are stumbling-blocks in the way of the world—yet they are cherished and adhered to with a reverential tenderness that is due only to God. A worn-out creed is good for nothing but historical purposes, and when these are answered it ought to go into the rag-bag. . . . We travel toward the dawn, and every man who reverences the past, simply because it is the past, worships toward the setting sun, and will find himself in darkness before he is aware. That is an irrational reverence which always looks up and never around—which is always in awe and never in delight—which exceedingly fears and quakes, and has no tender raptures—which places God at a distance and fails to recognize Him in the thousand forms that appeal to our sense of Beauty, and the thousand small voices that speak of His immediate presence."

It was to rid himself, and those like-minded with him, of the rags of outworn creeds, that through much tribulation he worked so strenuously to found the Memorial Church of Springfield, and even the formal statement of belief of that church retains some declarations that probably he would later have eliminated.

CHAPTER XII.

Publication of "Kathrina"—Dr. Holland's Doctrine of Art a Ministry—Sudden Death in October, 1881—Poetical Tributes of E. C. Stedman and Dr. Gladden.

In 1867 he published his poem "Kathrina," and again it was said the book violated the canons of art, in spite of which it at once attained an almost unprecedented sale, Longfellow's "Hiawatha" only having surpassed it, showing that a multitude of people found something in it that met their spiritual wants; but again those persons who could not separate the artist from the man could not make up their minds whether Dr. Holland had turned Unitarian or Catholic. Certain they were that he was not plain old-fashioned "orthodox."

Two years before this he had said in a lecture on "Art and Life:" "The multitude acknowledge that they know nothing of art. They see an old painting that they would hesitate to give a dollar for at an auction shop sold for a hundred guineas,—'a phantom of delight,' to critics and connoisseurs,—and they shake their heads in profound self-distrust.

They see a select few go into raptures over the long-drawn, dreary iterations and reiterations of a symphony, and confess that they know nothing of music. They read a literary performance which stirs and inspires them—which elevates and enlarges them—which fills them with delight and satisfaction, and are shocked and chagrined to learn, at the end of the month, by the shrewd critic of the review, that they have been so vulgar as to be pleased with something that tramples on every rule of art."

Just before "Kathrina" appeared, Taine had put forth his great work on art, in which he says: "Art can have no moral purpose"—and certainly it made no difference what form Dr. Holland's literary work took—editorial, lecture, story, or poem—there was always the sermon in it, and, to quote Mr. Gladden, "if Taine's dictum is true, then certainly Dr. Holland was not distinctively an artist; but then with equal certainty there is something higher than art. If the poem or the novel that sets forth the ideals of high morality, and urges man toward them, is in bad literary form, then Dr. Holland's work must be pronounced defective from the stand-point of criticism. . . . Dr. Holland had his own theory of literary art, a theory carefully worked out in 'Kathrina,' and it is very different from that of Taine. It was, in short, that art is not for pleasure but for ministry; that it is degraded and accursed when it finds no end beyond itself. The words of *Kathrina*, spoken to her husband, express the author's deliberate judgment on this point:

"'Every gift
That God bestows on men holds in itself
The secret of its office, like the rake
The gardener wields. The rake was made to till—
Was fashioned, head and handle, for just that;
And if, by grace of God you hold a gift
So fashioned and adapted, that it stands
In like relation of supremest use
To life of men, the office of your gift
Has perfect definition. Gift like this
Is yours, my husband. In your facile hands
God placed it for the service of himself
In service of your kind. Taking this gift
And using it for God and for the world,
In your own way and in your own best way;
Seeking for light and knowledge everywhere
To guide your careful hand, and opening wide
To spiritual influx all your soul
That so your Master may breathe into you,
And breathe His great life through you, in such forms
Of pure presentment as he gives you skill
To build withal—that's all of art—for you.
Art is an instrument, and not an end—
A servant, not a master, nor a god
To be bowed down to.'

"Holding that theory of literary art, whatever else you may say about him, you cannot deny that his methods were intelligently chosen and consistently followed. Of course there is nothing original in all this. The notion of what gifts are for is borrowed from a very old Book; it is the application to the work of the writer of the Master's 'I came not to be ministered unto, but to minister;' 'I am among you as he that serveth.' It is the Christian law and the Christian motive extended into the world of letters."

Life seemed to have brought all its affluence of enjoyment to Dr. Holland. All the dreams of his boyhood and all the aspirations of his ambitious youth had "come true." He was the owner of a beautiful home that had become one of the choice social centres of New York ; there he was surrounded by a family who delighted in him, and in the continued and cumulative success of his magazine. He had built his charming summer retreat of Bonnie-Castle, and had won a circle of admiring friends in the Thousand Islands community—his income was so ample that he could gratify every fancy, whether it was the buying of a boat or a fine picture, or the helping of a struggling congregation to build a commodious church—the cup of life seemed brimming over with delights, when from out the smiling skies there came a voice that he could not gainsay.

A sudden dart of the cruel pain called by the old pathologists a " breast-pang," most pathetic but accurate appellation, arrested his attention ; repeated, it sent him to an accomplished diagnostic specialist; "angina pectoris," he Latinized it, but the poor victim, having himself studied medicine, was deprived of any life-prolonging mystifications, and he clearly understood that though life might be prolonged by prudence, science has as yet found no cure for the trouble. No more lecturing—the nervous strain was too great—no sudden or violent effort, the pace henceforth must be with careful measured tread.

Every imaginative writer must find some isolation in which fancy can weave her fairy web, and every editor is beset with interruptions innumerable, and the men who combine the two must perforce have two "dens." Long before *Scribner's* had taken possession of its spacious quarters at Union Square, Dr. Holland had converted the top story of his house, where a billiard-room had been planned, into a library and workshop. Its outlook was to the east, and before a sunny window was planted a convenient work-a-day desk. In this quiet eyrie, above the noise and dust of the street, Dr. Holland wrote his "continued" stories and many of his "Topics of the Time." We fancy that at that desk he penned this from "Arthur Bonnicastle:" "Comfort of a certain sort there may be, in ease and in the gratification of that which is sensuous and sensual in human nature; but happiness is never a lazy man's dower, nor a sensualist's privilege. That is reserved for the worker, and can never be grasped and held, save by true manhood and true womanhood. It was a great lesson to learn, and it was learned for a lifetime; for, in this eventide of life, with the power to rest, I find no joy like that which comes to me at the table on which, day after day, I write the present record."

Immediately after what he called the reading of his death-warrant he resolutely set about arranging his business affairs, making his will, and extricating his assets from what may be called entanglement. His pastor at Alexandria Bay, to whom he was affectionately attached, writes: "His end was not on the morning when he died; it was in the four years of silent suffering, of imminent danger, of certain approaching death." Still he went undauntedly forth, looking death steadily in the face, and accomplishing each daily task precisely as if no shadow of a sword projected itself across the sunny window, whence he saw a world that seemed full of charms. He wrote to Mr. De Vries: "I trust if the change comes I may be ready for it. Life is so sweet and significant to me that, whenever I go I shall cast 'one loving, lingering, look behind.'"

On the afternoon of the 11th of October, 1881, he sat at his desk in the office of *Scribner's*, and was busily engaged in writing an article on President Garfield's death for the next issue of the magazine.

He had been so careful of his health that it was a long time since he had any sharp reminders of the tenuity of the silver cord, and on this afternoon had been to another floor of the building to see some of La Farge's fine productions in colored glass, and he declined an invitation to ride to his home, as he felt "just in the writing mood," and the last words he had penned might have been his own true epitaph. He said, referring to Garfield, "his sympathy with the humble drew to him the hearts of the world." His family thought him unusually bright and happy at the tea-table.

About six o'clock the next morning he wakened Mrs. Holland with a groan so piercing that it betrayed mortal agony, became unconscious, and before anyone else could reach him was gone.

"He passed through glory's morning gate
And woke in Paradise."

Was not this a true euthanasia? To-day, in the midst of the hurrying crowds that jostle each other in the streets of New York, and to-morrow, walking in the "green pastures and beside the still waters," led by the hand of the God in whom he had trusted utterly. To his family the shock was of the sort that no writing can ever describe, but after the terrible poignancy of the loss was assuaged by the gentle ministry of time they could see that it was

His biography is with the hunters above. To him the hearts of the world.

[Fac-simile of the last words written by Dr. Holland, October 11, 1881]

better thus. Possibly he would have chosen this way in spite of the instinctive recoil from "sudden death." There was no outward perceptible slow decay. He was in the plenitude of his mental powers and stood on the threshold of new plans, full of glorious promise, when God sent His swift, strong angel and rapt him from the sight of his beloved. Perhaps the sad pleasure of a final conscious "farewell" belongs more to the grieving survivors than to the parting soul; and in reviewing the career of this man, who in the sphere that God had marked out for him gave a ceaseless example of high living, we cannot but think that this swift summons was a merciful way of bringing him into the presence of that Master who to him was a living, daily, hourly inspiration and example.

The morning papers of October 12, 1881, on both sides of the ocean, brought the news to thousands of households that a voice to which they had loved to listen would be heard on earth thenceforth no more, and among many beautiful tributes, E. C. Stedman wrote that which aptly described the man and his parting.

J. G. H.

"Multis ille bonis flebilis occidit."—Hor., Carm., I., 24.

" Who knew him, loved him. His the longing heart
   For what his youth had missed, his manhood known—
  The haunts of Song, the fellowship of Art—
   And all their kin he strove to make his own.

> "But his the good true heart not thus content :
> The words that fireside groups at eve repeat,
> He spoke or sang : and far his sayings went,
> And simple households found his music sweet.
>
> "So Heaven was kind and gave him naught to grieve.
> Among his loved he woke at morn from rest—
> One smile—one pang—and gained betimes his leave
> Ere strength had lost its use, or life its zest."

On the Friday afternoon following, a simple funeral service was held in the dear earthly perfect home by Drs. Bevan and Murray, who had both been his pastors in the Brick Church, and then the "earthly house" was taken to Springfield, Mass., and laid by tender hands to rest amid the scenes that had witnessed his early struggles and his later triumphs, and in sight of the Mount Holyoke, that formed the mental background to all his early intellectual life. Dr. Gladden wrote of it—

> "Mountain that watchest down the vale
> Most like a couchant lion—
> Wide, winding river, whose fair breast
> Soft south winds gently die on—
> Lift up the head ; flow still and slow ;
> Let no chill blast now chide you ;
> For one who loved you long ago
> Lies down to sleep beside you.
>
> "You nursed within his boyish heart
> The springing love of beauty ;

You taught him, by your steadfast ways,
   The deeper love of duty ;
Your shade and shine about him lay
   In life's abundant labor ;
And now the mound that holds his dust
   Shall be your lowly neighbor.

" A good, brave man, a blameless man,
   He lived and wrought among us ;
The truth he taught, the tales he told,
   The heart-songs that he sung us,
All shine with white sincerity,
   All thrill with strong conviction ;
His words were seeds of honest deeds,
   His life a benediction.

" The art he loved was not the art
   That finds its end in pleasing ;
He loved to help and serve and bless
   With toil and care unceasing ;
No gift, he said, its fruit hath borne
   Until with love 'tis mated ;
No art is high, no art is pure,
   That is not consecrated.

" And thus, with kindly souls who pass
   Through Baca's vale of weeping,
Beside whose way the fountains play,
   Joy-bringing, verdure-keeping,
From strength to strength this pilgrim went,
   With grace that ne'er forsook him,
Till suddenly, at break of day,
   He was not, for God took him.

"We tell our loss, we bear our pain,
　　Still thankful hearts upraising—
For life so large and fruit so fair
　　Our God the giver praising.
The heart must bleed, the tears must fall,
　　But smiles through tear-drops glitter;
We drink the cup, and grateful find
　　The sweet within the bitter.

"O mountain! guard his precious dust;
　　O river! seaward flowing,
By night your softest dews bestow
　　To keep the grasses growing
That ever, with the bitter sweet
　　His sacred grave shall cover—
Servant of man and friend of God,
　　Brave thinker, steadfast lover."

October 11, 1881.

During the summer previous to his death he had been much interested and engrossed in the preparations making for the marriage of his oldest daughter to Mr. John Kasson Howe, of Troy, N. Y., which was to take place in the autumn, and Helen Hunt—many of whose precious poems were first printed in *Scribner's*, wrote on the day of his death:

I.

"We may not choose! Ah, if we might, how we
Should linger here, not ready to be dead,
Till one more loving thing were looked, or said—
Till some dear child's estate of joy should be

Complete—or we, triumphant, late, should see
Some great cause win, for which our hearts had bled—
Some hope come true which all our lives had fed—
Some bitter sorrow fade away and flee,
Which we, rebellious, had too bitter thought;
Or even—so our human hearts would cling,
If but they might, to this fair world inwrought
With heavenly beauty in each smallest thing—
We would refuse to die till we had sought
One violet more, heard one more robin sing!

II.

"We may not choose; but if we did foreknow
The hour when we should pass from human sight,
What words were last that we should say, or write,
Could we pray fate a sweeter boon to show
Than bid our last words burn with loving glow
Of heart-felt praise, to lift, and make more bright
A great man's memory, set in clearer light?
Ah yes! Fate could one boon more sweet bestow:—
So frame those words that every heart which knew
Should, sudden, awe-struck, weeping turn away
And cry: 'His own hand his best wreath must lay!
Of his own life his own last words are true—
So true, love's truth no truer thing can say—
"By sympathy all hearts to him he drew." ' "

Helen Hunt Jackson was born six miles from where Dr. Holland first opened his eyes upon life. Her father was a distinguished professor in Amherst College—a brilliant member of the "New

England Brahmin caste"—when the obscure boy's heart was bitter from the obstructed ambition that in vain urged him toward entering the classic halls of the college. It is an instructive comment on the allotments of human destiny that, long years after, the professor's gifted child should bring her literary productions—each one "a gem of purest ray"—to this foreordained editor for judgment and publication. She found in him a sympathetic friend as well as an appreciative literary judge. As her mind ripened, and still more, as she consciously approached the shores of the silent sea—and, looking backward over the track already passed, she weighed things justly—she said, "Only what I have done with a moral purpose seems now of any worth to me," and she found it possible to fully read and estimate a character and career whose pre-eminent distinction was the exaltation of the moral.

CHAPTER XIII.

Memorial Services—In Springfield, New York, Alexandria Bay, and Belchertown—Eulogies of Edward Eggleston, George S. Merriam, and Others—Dr. Bevan's Sermon—Discourse of Rev. P. W. Lyman.

ON the Sunday evening after the burial (October 16th) a Memorial Service was held in the Memorial Church of Springfield, of which he had been one of the founders when it required high moral courage to be a positive and aggressive "founder." Now, after sixteen years, the thought of the world had broadened and risen, approximately, to the place where he had stood then, and men of all creeds and callings came together to do honor to a stainless memory. Dr. Eustis, pastor of the church, conducted the services, assisted by Rev. Dr. Terhune, Rev. J. W. Harding, and Rev. Dr. Gladden. A letter of regret from Rev. Dr. R. H. Seeley, of Haverhill, and a telegram from President Porter, of Yale, both former pastors of Dr. Holland, were read. Dr. Eustis said that Dr. Holland was a remarkably successful man; that during his life he had accomplished nearly every desire of his heart. But there was one that was not gratified, namely, that he might write a hymn which should be sung in all the churches. He proposed that the Thanksgiving hymn from "Bitter-Sweet," sung to the tune of "Duke Street," would be a worthy one to sing on the present occasion.

> "For summer's bloom and autumn's blight,
>   For bending wheat and blasted maize,
>   For health and sickness, Lord of light
>   And Lord of darkness, hear our praise.
>
> "We trace to Thee our joys and woes—
>   To Thee of causes still the cause :
>   We thank Thee that Thy hand bestows ;
>   We bless Thee that Thy love withdraws.
>
> "We bring no sorrows to Thy throne ;
>   We come to Thee with no complaint,
>   In Providence Thy will is done,
>   And that is sacred to the saint."

The Rev. Dr. Buckingham was the pastor who had advised Dr. Holland to go to the North Church in 1854, as a place where his influence would tell more powerfully than in the very thoroughly established and conservative church over which he was himself then settled. Among other things Dr. Buckingham called attention to his services as the leader of the choir, in their essential element of an act of praise, and said he was a pure-minded, conscientious and useful church member, and all who have ever been associated with him in such relations can bear the freest testimony in this respect to his singular simplicity, to his tender piety, to his conscientious fidelity, and generous liberality in all the relations he sustained to these churches, and to religious effort in this city. It should be noted that while he was jealous of the religious liberty of others, and championed their claims so manfully, he never needed indulgence for heresy of his own. He believed in the Bible, and he adored and trusted in Jesus Christ as the only Saviour of men.

Mr. George S. Merriam said: "It was the especial distinction of Dr. Holland that he used the newspaper's power to serve the preacher's purpose. As a moral teacher he found a weapon superior to the old, as a rifle is superior to a cross-bow, or a locomotive to a stage-coach. No less did he enlarge and ennoble the function of journalism by putting it to a new and higher use. He showed that a newspaper might do something more than tell the news; something besides discuss what is doing at Washington; something more, even, than to act as guide and judge in literature and art and public affairs. He used the daily or the monthly journal to purify and sweeten the fountains of personal and family life. . . . He was faithful to the light that was in him; he was open-eyed and sensitive to the conditions of the time; he met the opportunity as it offered; and thus he did what was given him to do. He did a work large in itself, large in the impress it left on two great periodicals; large as the omen of the nobler work to be done by the press, an instance of the new and greater channels through which God fulfils his purposes."

Dr. Eggleston, who had known him intimately as the editor-in-chief of *Scribner's*, traced the connection between the later growth of Dr. Holland and the vicissitudes of his early life: "He had despairingly thought in his young manhood that the world had no place for him; had tried several things and failed, like many a young man passing through similar struggles to-day, who is destined to play an important part in the world. People often wonder that they have not recognized such men before. It is always perfectly safe to be kind and not to snub a young and ambitious man. We should make a little smoother and a little sweeter and better, if we can, the pathway of a struggling, ambitious, and sensitive young man, such as Dr. Holland was in those earlier years. The trials of this period, however, only served to strengthen and develop the man."

Mr. Roswell Smith—his coadjutor in establishing the Magazine—said, in part: "Dr. Holland was a man who decided the most important questions with almost lightning rapidity. I never saw a man whose decisions on important questions were so instantaneous. He used to say, 'I put my confidence in men rather than things.'

"Dr. Holland knew that he had often been charged with a want of orthodoxy. He used to repeat with zest the story of a Springfield clergyman who, when absent from home, was asked what were Dr. Holland's religious opinions. 'Have you read Dr. Holland's books and can you not learn his beliefs there?' The answer was, 'Yes, I've read his books, but first I come across something that makes me think he is a Unitarian, and then I read on and find something that leads me to think that he is a "Christian!"' . . . Dr. Holland appreciated the fact that he was a misunderstood man, and that he was credited with holding sentiments and the advocating of views that he thoroughly abhorred; and one motive, he said, in starting a literary magazine was, that he might set himself right on the record.

"No man held the clerical profession in higher esteem than Dr. Holland. Indeed his estimate of it was so high and his desire that it should attain the highest usefulness was such that it led him to be impatient with its defects; and the same is true of his love for the Church, and his respect for the prayer-meeting. He felt that these were the hope of the world, and he could not tolerate stupidity or intolerance in either the one or the other. Ministers had no truer friend than he, and very many of them recognized it and held him in the highest regard. No minister ever came to him to consult him about leaving his chosen profession and going into literature, or into any other pursuit, but Dr. Holland turned him back and exhorted him with the greatest earnestness to stick to the preaching of the gospel as the highest earthly calling.

"The whole generation of men of the age of Dr. Gladden, Dr. Eggleston, and myself, who were ten years younger than Dr. Holland, read his earlier works with the greatest interest, and we feel that we owe to him a debt of gratitude which we can never repay for the influence he exercised upon our lives."

On the same evening in which this general Memorial Service was held, and at which his poem was read, Dr. Gladden preached a memorial sermon in the church with which Dr. Holland had been united for eleven years, from the text, "I am among you as he that serveth." After having dwelt upon all the services rendered in his capacity of committee-man and general promoter of the interests of the church he spoke of Dr. Holland's singing :

"It was quite evident to one who saw and heard him singing, that it was something more than a performance—that it was worship." After a careful estimate of his literary work, and in answer to some of the critics, Dr. Gladden said: "At any rate, it is enough to say that he understood what he was about when he wrote novels with a purpose. And it must be admitted by everybody that his purposes were high and pure; that the blows he struck with this good weapon of fiction were telling blows. The same thing is true of his poems. All of his principal poems take hold of great themes, deal with the great interests of character and the great spiritual laws. We may not agree with him in all the lessons that he seeks to teach in these poems—I own that I do not;—but we cannot deny the lofty purpose and the earnest thought that pulsate through them all. Whatever we may say of their philosophy, the spirit that animates them is large and free.

"When I thus exalt the moral and religious element that characterizes all that Dr. Holland wrote, I would not wish to be understood as denying to his stories and poems that quality which the pagan critics insist upon, the power of giving pleasure; not only in the felicitous and picturesque rhetoric and the stirring music of his words, but also in his quick insight into character, and his happy delineations of men and manners he has delighted a great multitude of readers. In his stories especially, while he has always aimed at some high purpose, he has succeeded in imparting a great deal of pleasure, not only to those who read for the plot, but also to those who enjoy the unfolding of character and the representation of life.

"He had a quick and sure intuition of the consciousness of his time. He knew what men were thinking about. He discerned the difficulties of the average thinker, the problems with which he was struggling, and he knew how, with deft and homely phrase, to put him on the track of a right solution. This was one great secret of his success as a writer and, especially, as an editor. . . . To all these problems he brought not only a shrewd common-sense, but an uncompromising idealism. 'Ideals,' he said, 'are the world's masters.' . . . That which is godlike in men goes ahead of them, into some form of their own choosing, to beckon them toward perfection and to lead them toward God. Certainly this was true of him. His ideals of right, and truth, and purity ruled all his thinking, shaped all his teaching.

"He was a true and generous friend. With quick sympathies and warm enthusiasms, he was always ready to bear the burdens of others, and his hearty words and painstaking services have lightened many a heart.

"But I shall sum up all, and explain all when

I say that Dr. Holland was a Christian man. The sincere and manly faith in God, and in his Son Jesus Christ, which he was never ashamed to confess, was the plastic force by which his character was formed, his purposes were shaped. All that I have said about him is but an expansion of this sentence. . . . He was a servant of the Master who went about doing good. . . . With the people whose religion is nothing but 'orthodoxy,' to whom the formularies of doctrine are more than the fruits of character, he found it hard to have patience. 'A Christianity which consists only of opinions,' he said not long ago, 'is a very shabby article, and we do not pretend to believe in it. The Christianity which is a divine life, a divine inspiration, and a divine hope is so inexpressibly dear to so many people, it is such a help to them in their struggles with their grosser nature, it gives to life and to death so stupendous a meaning, it is such a comfort in trouble and sorrow and in burden-bearing, that we should need to be inhuman not to regard the efforts aimed at its overthrow as aimed at the dearest interests of the human race.' It was because he believed with such unconquerable faith in Christianity as a life and an experience that his wrath was kindled against the men who sought to dessicate it into formulas, and to cast out of the Church all holy and saintly servants of Christ who cannot chew these theological chips. For the ringing words that he has uttered in defence of the liberty that always ought to be, where the Spirit of the Lord is, the Church of God remains his debtor."

On the following Sunday the pastor of the church at Alexandria Bay preached a memorial sermon in the church, that had been greatly enlarged and beautified during the preceding summer, largely through Dr. Holland's liberality. The text was, "Mark the perfect man, and behold the upright, for the end of that man is peace." In commenting on Dr. Holland's character as exhibited in his summer home, he said: "There you found the stern qualities that characterize the man blended with the gentler that form the woman. . . . Dr. Holland was true as steel, but transparent as crystal. . . . When you looked on that kindly countenance, into that clear, open eye, you felt, more than understood, that that eye was the mirror of a truthful soul ; that there was sincerity, simplicity, complete guilelessness. He knew no meanness; all trickery was utterly foreign to him ; if necessary, he would, as David has it, swear to his own hurt and change not. And that truth-loving soul hated all kinds of falsehood and injustice. Though he sought to save the sinner, yet he condemned his sin. . . . During the four years of my connection with Dr. Holland, I have often likened him to John, the apostle of love. He adorned the doctrine of Christ with all the gentler graces.

"Of his love to human-kind I need not speak. . . . He once said to me, 'I have worked every day for forty years and worked hard.' . . . That busy brain of his was always observing, always taking in actual life; the street, the store, the office, were his school, and that busy pen of his hurried over the paper to give lessons to millions of souls. . . . Often and eloquently did he preach sermons to millions—sermons that must have saved lost sons and lost daughters, . . . and to all he taught the true philosophy of faith, the true way of life. And all this because of his love of God. The love of God was with him the beginning and the end. The word of God was his book of life; the house of God a house of feasting; the people of God his brothers and sisters; the day of the Lord a day of rest and gladness. His presence in the sanctuary was an inspiration to his pastor and to all that could see him. To hear him sing in that melodious tenor, so distinctly pronouncing every word with that deep feeling and wonderful pathos, was a delight to the ear, but more so to the soul. One day, singing that beautiful hymn, 'Gentle Jesus, how I love thee!' I was struck with the pathos in his singing. The way in which he sang it—the deep feeling, the tearful eye—were a revelation of the Christ-loving soul within. . . . He enjoyed life, his life-work was yielding precious rewards; he had all that life could give, and he had every faculty unimpaired, keen, and healthy to enjoy it. Then there came the messenger, saying, 'Prepare thy house, for thou shalt die;' and his answer, not in so many words but in every action was, 'Lord, I am ready; thy time is my time; thy will is my will.' . . . Therefore let us build a memorial in this place, not only of marble in this house, but of Christian manhood in our hearts, in our homes, in our churches, in our community, and thus render thanks unto God who gave, who hath taken away, whose name be blessed forevermore."

During the summer just then passed Dr. Holland had written a poem concerning a favorite dog —a beautiful white setter that had become very familiar to the eyes of the Alexandria Bay folk, as his constant companion. After a tender tribute to the loving fidelity of this dog, he closes in the most characteristic way:

> "Ah, Blanco! did I worship God,
> As truly as you worship me,
> Or follow where my Master trod,
> With your humility;

"Did I sit fondly at his feet,
  As you, dear Blanco, sit at mine,
  And watch him with a love as sweet,
My life would grow divine."

After the congregation had assembled for the memorial service, and the minister had named the object of the meeting, and spoken of the lost benefactor and friend, this dog entered the church, walked up and down the aisles, looked at the preacher, as much as to say "Where?" and went back. It was but a trifling incident, that under other circumstances would have been considered a disturbing intrusion; as it was, it brought the quick tears to many unused eyes.

On the Sabbath evening succeeding the one where those who had seen how a summer sojourner can take his religion with him into the country, and leave an impression of its vivifying power, Dr. Bevan preached a carefully prepared memorial discourse in the Brick Church, in New York, which had been elaborately draped in black as a testimonial to the loss this church felt in the death of the man who had faithfully borne his share in both the temporalities and the spiritualities of the church work for the eleven years since he had cast in his Christian lot with them.

Dr. Bevan's texts were, "He that handleth a matter wisely shall find good; and whoso trusteth in the Lord, happy is he;" and, "A word fitly spoken is like apples of gold in pictures of silver."

He said: "I shall not easily forget the shock caused by the announcement of the death of Dr. Holland. . . . On the Sunday morning previous to his death he took his place in the church, and there, just beneath the pulpit, I saw the grave and earnest countenance, the tender and responsive eyes. Perhaps a little graver than usual was the face, and perhaps as I now recall the eyes there was a shadow that thinly veiled the light of his outlooking. And yet this may be only the fancy born of our present knowledge that death was already at his heels, and that the communion service at which he was present, on that last Sabbath morning, was soon to be followed by the summons to enter into the higher communion of the saints in light. In the full strength of his mental powers—with the one exception of those attacks of pain which exertion brought on, all his bodily activities unabated, having gained a place of wide reputation and large significance, wielding the peculiar influence of a popular magazine, conceiving the plans of new labor, to accomplish which he felt himself more able than at any time; and yet with work done and rounded off with noteworthy completeness, the call came, and in a moment he disappeared from the eyes of love and comradeship, and the watch of fellow-toilers, and has left behind a pure memory, a good record, a healthy inspiration, a name of strength. It is useful as it is becoming to endeavor to understand something of such a man's life, to hear the voice that speaks from the story of character and achievement which a true man leaves for us to read ; for, you may be sure, brethren, that God sends a message by each man's conduct and being. The canon of the inspired word of good living is never closed. And if men are wise who can read the signs of the times, surely there is a wisdom which the children of wisdom will justify, in studying the truth that God has made known and illustrated in these sacraments and symbols of highest work—the lives of good men."

After sketching the main facts of a career less familiar to Brick Church people, in virtue of their being New Yorkers, than to New England men, Dr. Bevan showed a side of life and character that we sometimes sadly miss in men of letters. "Busy and absorbed as was Dr. Holland's life in the labors of the writer, he was by no means so occupied as to leave no place for those other duties, private and social, which go to make up the fulness and completeness of our career. Into the privacy of the domestic scene I will not intrude ; but many of you know what a husband and father and friend this man was. Nowhere did his fine form and countenance appear to better advantage than in dispensing the courtesies of social life, and he ever loved to gather around him, not only those who were admitted to the inner sanctities of personal affection, but the circles which represented all shades of opinion and all types of culture and activity.

"He never neglected the duties of public worship, and bore his share of those labors which sustain and develop the church, . . . and his relation to the church did not become less intimate as he grew in wealth and influence. Very often men who in their early days are good churchmen, when they achieve earthly success retire, at least from the more manifest and practical service of religion. . . . Surely the work of the Lord is not that which should suffer at the hands of those whom the Lord is blessing. It was thus our friend lived and labored. Always a pure, true, brave man; always at his post; always kindly sympathetic, helpful, he fell with a fame and reputation which no man might be unwilling to claim.

"That Dr. Holland's course was one of success no one will for a moment doubt. If a man's first business in life is to provide things honest in the sight of all men, both for himself and his family, then, certainly, viewed from that point of human necessity, we can congratulate our friend upon his achievement.

"It is not often that the mere man of letters succeeds in secular things with a more marked success; and when we ask ourselves the cause of it, we find, apart from the skill with which he did his work, the influence of those protecting and conserving virtues which are the security and glory of life.

"When Oliver Goldsmith died, leaving debts of $10,000 unpaid, Dr. Johnson gently said, 'Never was poet so trusted,' and there has come a sort of popular expectation that a man of letters shall be in some way a Bohemian, and shall especially make a wreck of health, and social virtue, and family standing. . . . Dr. Holland understood how to husband his means. . . . His views about the use of intoxicating drinks were well known, and he endured a kind of reproach and social martyrdom from the very fact of his total abstinence. And yet who shall impugn his motives, or lessen for a moment the esteem in which we regard his social and hospitable qualities? None found him less genial because he did not look upon the wine when it was red, when it giveth its color in the cup. And how many a famous name in letters and in song might have been spared the shame and obloquy which tender affection has to hide, if the example of Holland had been followed, and there had been the exercise of that self-restraint by which he was preserved!

"And what might I not say, were this other than a public occasion, as to the domestic relations of our friend? He had ambition; he loved fame; he delighted in the honor men gave him; he enjoyed the pleasant things which money could afford. But all these were chiefly cared for that he might crown the days and make bright the life of the woman he had chosen in his youth, and the dear hearts God had given them in their union of confidence and love. He was a home-lover and a home-keeper. He knew the glory and strength of a nation was in the fidelity of husband and wife, and in the sweet joys of the fireside. . . . Read his books, peruse his essays, con his songs, recall his conversations, and you will recognize how the man was every whit of him a man of virtue, of probity, of pureness, and self-restraint, and there you will find the secret of that success which not only gained, but kept, which was not only fame, but also character; which was built not upon the shifting sands of a fickle popularity, but upon the strong, firm foundation of a personal and a domestic virtue.

"Holland was a good man. Nothing illustrated this more than the spirit with which he dealt with certain forms of life and letters as seen in our times, or as recorded in the past. . . . He was large-hearted and broad in his views. Some people have thought him latitudinarian, almost too willing to allow a scope and liberty which might become license and absence of all law. . . . And yet he gave no indulgence to licentious forms of art in any sort. In plain nervous speech he rebuked excesses and abuses of every kind. The artist, in Holland's estimation, was always less than an artist when he forgot the laws of morality and virtue. In poetry, in painting, in prose, in sculpture, in politics, in social life, everywhere he sought to purify and to ennoble the aims of men. . . . And the real explanation of all this was the religious nature that lay at the base of his character. . . . He was a Christian man in the deepest sense of that term. . . . Christian teaching had not stiffened with him into a hard dogma of inflexible belief, to be used rather as a test of other people's opinions and life than the inspiration of his own. Neither had religious truth become for him a sort of social conscience, a kind of historical, mental, and spiritual atmosphere which a man was to take on, without finding in it much personal significance; indeed, on the whole, thinking it advisable not greatly to inquire, lest the very elements and combinations of faith, subjective, if not objective, might be rudely disturbed. But religion had been to him a sore disquietude.[*] The truth of Christ and his Gospel had been painfully questioned by him at one time. He passed through a critical and doubtful season, and this, let it be noted, with no light heart. He did not think scepticism and questioning and uncertainty a fine thing, or a trifling matter. But it was with tears, and strong cries, and deep misgivings that he made his way through the dark valley and at last came into the light that was beyond. Historic and parental and social and national religion thus became personal with Dr. Holland, and hence it was a fire that consumed him—a fountain within that must have found its way and poured forth its stream. It was this that caused some of Dr. Holland's words to seem to some people to be dangerous and novel. Men who go through these crises of spiritual history, as he went through, will generally emerge with a few truths clearly apprehended, vital, all inspiring; and for the rest they will have a respectful honor but no very passionate regard. Such men learn, if I may so call it, the perspective of religion. The system of doctrine is not quite a wooden puzzle, the smallest peg of which is the key and binder of the whole. The panorama of divine truth is not represented after the fashion of Chinese art, where each object is painted as if the artist was close to it and saw nothing else. But he had allowed for himself many things to pass into a secondary place, and to be wholly subordinate to the grand and central facts of God his Father and Jesus Christ his Saviour. That he was devout, a humble believer in Jesus

Christ, accepting the Gospel of the Crucified One as the only hope of the world, no man who had preached to Dr. Holland for five years and had seen his face as the mysteries of the kingdom were proclaimed, and had drawn inspiration from that rapturous countenance, could for a moment doubt. . . .

"Had he worked on the lower plane of careless ethics, he would not have been the writer, the poet, the novelist that he became. The Divine Artist himself has created a world infinitely more wonderful and fair, because beyond the material form, the intellectual fitness, the natural beauty, there were ends of righteousness and goodness that have lifted earth to heaven and made man to become a son of God. Here the popular heart and conscience have more insight than the critic. The negative morality of the artist will sink him to the narrow sphere of a school. The ethics of art will raise it to be the religion of the race. . . . If he was an ideal man, he had found that ideal in the Christian life. His thoughts, his workings, were all inspired by his Christian life and character—his character a fresh testimony to the truth and power of that Gospel which makes wise unto salvation — that religion which has the promise of the life that now is, and of that which is to come."

Another very tender and beautiful tribute was paid his memory, on the Sunday after his death, in his native town of Belchertown, Mass., in a discourse by the Rev. P. W. Lyman, in which, in addition to the main facts connected with his spiritual life and Christian character, he summed up the amount of his literary work in books thus: "It is no small accomplishment to put eighteen different volumes of good literature upon the world's book-shelves; books, too, of such intrinsic merit, and such pertinence to the wants of men, that every one of them was a business success, and that upward of five-hundred thousand volumes, all told, have already been paid for by the public. In this respect certainly his success has been unequalled among Americans. The writer of these books has talked about things concerning which men wished to hear. He has talked in a way to meet their general approval. . . .

"The editorial chair of a magazine whose readers approximate a million is a responsible place. The opportunity of speaking each month, as the recognized editor, to such a vast and noble constituency, on themes occupying their thought and calling for their action, gave Dr. Holland a grip on the world's life which he used for the world's advantage; for, as the *Tribune* well says, 'Whenever a question had a right and a wrong side, he was always found on the right. If he gave advice, it was almost always good.'

"Dr. Holland was not only a literary man, he

was also a social force. He was the centre of a cultured and admiring circle of whose friendship he was justly proud. That influential circle saw and felt the beauty and value of his Christian life. He rejoiced in his social opportunities, and, through all his use of them, his high moral and Christian purpose runs: he courageously and consistently used both his social and his literary vantage-ground to advance the theory and practice of total abstinence from all alcoholic beverages. Some of his most effective work was in that line. He was an unsparing enemy of the social glass. To the wine-drinking customs of respectable society he gave no quarter.

"In regard to political and social abuses, he has often spoken in no measured terms. In the same spirit in which he wrote his essay on the 'Canonization of the Vicious,' after the downfall of Tweed and the death of Fisk, he wrote his article on 'Easy Lessons from Hard Lives.' He cautioned his readers against the feeling that Fisk was any better man because he was killed. He protested against the destructive doctrine of those who would forbid the novelist, as material for his art, the great questions which concern the life and prosperity of individuals and society.

"Dr. Holland felt that his use of fiction as a vehicle of moral and religious truth was sanctioned fully by the Scripture statement: 'And without a parable spake he not to them.' Christ and his commands were an ever-present inspiration, and were the informing soul of his literary work. He said in one of his latest 'Topics,' 'That which is best and most poetic in human life has uniformly grown out of the motives born of faith in spiritual things. The greatest heroisms that have illustrated the history of the human race, and have thus become an inspiration in our literature, have been born of faith in things unseen. The loves that have made life divine, the self-devotion that has made life beautiful, the transformations of character which have illuminated the beneficent power of religion, the high moralities that have given safety and purity and dignity to society, the aspirations that have gone heavenward from a world of conscious imperfection, all these are the natural outcome of faith in the spiritual world.'"

CHAPTER XIV.

Dr. Holland's Will—Tribute of his Associates in the Magazine Editorship—The Secular Press on his Power and its Sources—Tribute of the Religious Papers—His Family, Grave, and Monument.

It certainly is reassuring in this day of analyzing doubt, and shallow, conceited scepticism, to note how the poets—Whittier, Tennyson, Browning—have clung to, and iterated and reiterated their faith in God and immortality; their unalterable belief that the soul of man was made for an ever-progressive upward destiny; it is they

> "Whose voices ring out a world's message
> Unflinching, uplifting, and true."

In one of his Easter "Topics" he said: "A living religion never could have been founded on a dead Christ; and it is safe to say that a religion that rests on a living Christ can never be superseded or destroyed;" and this belief led him into active Christian labor and fellowship wherever he lived, and made him a leading spirit in any church with which he was connected, for nothing would persuade him that a man could be as good a Christian out of the church as in it. He believed in a man's showing his colors, and standing up to be counted "for Christ," and he did all that he could, everywhere, to bring Christ to men, and men to Christ, and knowing himself to be no pharisee or hypocrite, he cared not if men of another type called him "prig;" and the crucial test of such a faith as his came in those four long years in which he looked death steadily in the face, and went quietly forward with his daily work as calmly as if the impending summons were merely the request of a messenger for him to step into an adjoining room.

He had written "Arthur Bonnicastle," while yet in the possession of high health; but in it he said: "The generations come and go without significance, if there be not the confident hope and expectation of something to follow, so grand, so sweet, and beautiful, that we can look upon it without pain or misgiving; faith draws the poison from every grief, takes the sting from every loss, and quenches the fire of every pain; and only faith can do it."

The calmness with which he worked on, taking as keen and deep an interest in all the living issues of the day as if he were to have an immortality on earth, and see them all carried to their ultimate conclusions, was not the result of indifference, but intelligent conviction, and it was but a short time before the silver cord gave way that he wrote "Threnody," of which this extract shows the ground of the quietness that possessed his soul:

> "O life! why art thou so bright a boon?
> O breath! why art thou so sweet?
> O friends! how can you forget so soon
> The loved ones that lie at your feet?
>
> "The ways of men are busy and bright,
> The eye of woman is kind;
> It is sweet for the eyes to behold the light,
> But the dying and dead are blind.
>
> "And the world goes round and round,
> And the sun falls into the sea,
> And whether I'm on, or under the ground,
> The world cares little for me.
>
> "But if life awake, and will never cease,
> On the future distant shore,
> And the rose of love, and the lily of peace,
> Shall bloom there for evermore—
>
> "Let the world go round and round
> And the sun sink into the sea,
> For whether I'm on, or under the ground,
> Oh! what will it matter to me."

He added to the testimony of an actively consistent life in the service of Christ this deliberate declaration in his will: "I am thankful for having enjoyed the privileges of labor and influence, thankful for wife and children, thankful for all my successes. I have intentionally and consciously wronged no man, and if I know my heart I have forgiven all my enemies. For the great hereafter I trust in the Infinite Love, as it is expressed to me in the life and death of my Lord and Saviour Jesus Christ."

Well might he be grateful for his opportunity of influence. The newspaper and the magazine hold to-day the dominant power in the moulding of public opinion which in the last century pertained to the clergy and the pulpit. The first issue of *Scribner's* was 40,000 copies, and long before its first editor died it had attained a circulation of 150,000 a month, and in the eleven years in which Dr. Holland wrote his "Topics" not less than 10,000,000 copies were printed. Well might he rejoice in the power to plant pure and just and pertinent thoughts on the subjects that were engrossing them in the minds of *the people*, those people who there often found "a way out" in perplexity, or an uplifting inspiration to keep on some chosen and worthy course; and among all these millions of words not one that could contaminate or poison or mislead into devious paths. Surely when God denied his mother's darling wish, he was leading him by a way which he knew not. He left two "Topics" ready for the next issue—that next issue that always haunts the editor.

A copy of the first issue of the magazine under its new name of *The Century*, and in its quaint present style of cover, was put into his hands a few days before his death. There was no presentiment that his work was done in the "Topics"—"Political Education" and "Literary Eccentricity"—that occupy his department in the last number of *Scribner's*. There was a singular completeness in the last and greatest of the "successes," for which he was grateful. It was exactly eleven years since the first lavender-colored issue had made its appearance, bearing his name on the cover and title-page, and the twenty-two bound volumes stand in hundreds of libraries, the successive "Topics" containing a complete reflection of the "Times," so that in a certain sense he has built an enduring monument with his own hand, for in future times the historian and the antiquarian will come to these volumes to learn what it was that interested us of this nineteenth century, and the direct, simple, pure, rhythmical English of the unsensational style in which they are treated will charm, and hold the attention of the reader, and give to them a permanent literary value.

In one of Robertson's sermons he says: "There is one honest hour in which a man's character and career is justly judged by both friends and enemies. It is the time which intervenes between his death and burial," and when the man who has fallen belongs to the great guild of editors the judgment finds itself recorded in the next issue of newspaper or magazine. *The Century* for December, 1881 (the November number was printed before he died), contained a careful estimate of the *man* as he appeared to those who had come into daily contact with him for longer or shorter periods during the past eleven years, and it is quite certain that the hands who recorded the judgments were of men who had "summered and wintered with him."

Mr. Eggleston says: "Doctor Holland was a man of dignified and impressive presence; he had something of that talent for affairs that is indispensable to the journalist, but he was also a man of rare simplicity and transparency. He often showed his inmost thoughts to strangers and cast the pearls of his confidence before swine who turned upon him. He loved approbation and he craved affection. De Quincey never got over the physical pangs occasioned by prolonged hunger, and the man who has been thoroughly brow-beaten and down-trodden by persistent hard fortune in his growth is likely to have a life-long hunger for the love and appreciation of his fellows. This appetite for approval, joined to a nature incorrigibly frank and open, made Dr. Holland seem to some people to possess more self-esteem than he really had. In truth a great deal of what appeared to be self-assertion was the offspring of a latent self-discouragement. No critic could make a more acute estimate of Dr. Holland's ethical books than he does in these modest words from the preface to 'Lessons in Life':

"'In this book, as in its predecessors, the author has aimed at being neither brilliant nor profound. He has endeavored simply to treat in a familiar and attractive way a few of the more prominent questions which concern the life of every thoughtful man and woman. Indeed, he can hardly pretend to have done more than organize and put into form the average thinking of those who read his books, to place before the people the sum of their own choicer judgments, and he neither expects nor wishes for these essays higher praise than that which accords to them the quality of common-sense.'

"Having been poor himself he gave freely to others who were straitened. His generosity, and what I have denominated his simplicity, made him a prey to the ingenious romancers who live upon the sympathies of the good. He said once that he could better afford to give a worthless fellow twenty-five dollars than to subject himself to the demoralizing influences of suspicion. It gave him a severe pang to distrust anybody.

"After all, the great heart was a large part of the man. He cherished high and generous ideals himself and nourished them in others. His sympathies and sensibilities nothing could blunt. He had words of kindness for the humblest, and he loved the common people with a sympathy which reacted upon his own life and character. He would sometimes, at Bonnie-Castle, hide his face in his hands, with a sort of terror, when he saw strangers approaching, but he would never refuse to see them and show them about the place. His superabundant sympathy drew to him, from all classes of society, a love not often given to any man. People visited his summer home as though making a pilgrimage to a shrine, and carried away relics of every kind, begging sometimes even for a handful of pebbles out of the roadway. This grateful love of thousands grew out of the genuine service that he had been able to render to the men and women of his generation, and it was a noble and enviable guerdon, bravely and worthily won."

Another hand in *The Century* establishment wrote: "He had accomplished nearly every desire of his heart. His life had grown broader and richer to its close. Though keenly sensitive to sharp criticism, and often suffering from it, still he was buoyed up through all his busy career by the grateful affections of untold thousands, and the love of all who were near him. He lived long enough not only to be able to say honestly that he had forgiven all his enemies, but long enough to gain the reverence and attachment of those who had planted the deepest thorns in his side. . . .

"It is hard to do here, in these columns, for our lamented chief, what he has so often done for his own comrades stricken down at his side. . . . Enough for us to say that the spirit of sympathy and helpfulness, that courtesy and gentle consideration which were so deeply characteristic of his published writings and his dealings with all, friends or utter strangers, with whom he came in contact; enough to say that these qualities of his heart had endeared him to his editorial and business associates in a peculiar manner. Every one of them remembers not only the uniform and unfailing gentleness of his manner, but also many acts of especial and extraordinary tenderness and forbearance. Even in cases where the springs of action must have been hard for him to understand, he still trusted; never once did he knowingly give pain to those beneath him in authority. He trusted his associates, and all employed in the work of the magazine, with a completeness that not only helped each to develop to the utmost his individual capacity, but which attached all of them to him in the bonds of personal affection and devoted loyalty. His quick sympathy, his warm encouragement, the inspiration of his generous confidence, his winning and fatherly presence, all these we shall miss beyond words."

Of course every leading newspaper had an article, more or less carefully written, containing an estimate, more or less just, of the elements and value of his literary work.

"Warrington," the brilliant Boston correspondent of the *Springfield Republican*, whose literary judgments were often "bitten" in with aqua-fortis, had said of him: "Holland does know how to set an intellectual table that will suit the mass of mankind," and it is interesting to see how the consensus of opinion, in the full chorus of newspaperdom, echoed this judgment.

Said the New York *Evening Mail*: "The influence of Dr. Holland has been vast, and his worth as a man has been almost beyond praise. The death of few American writers would cause sorrow in more hearts."

The *St. Louis Spectator* said: "Especially do the young people of America mourn his loss, for to them he was a good adviser and a dear friend."

The *St. Louis Globe-Democrat* said: "In all the sensational whirl of his time, which upset so many heads and touched so many pens with loose and doubtful messages, he stood his ground without a hint of flattery, and was at the last as at the first, an artist who scorned to lower his ideal. . . . The gossips will find no scandals clinging to his memory, and no account of regretful foibles to be condoned as the eccentricities of genius."

The *Chicago Standard* said: "His books have given pleasure and profit to thousands upon thousands of readers," while the *Colorado Gazette* dwelt on his conscientiousness.

It must be remembered that the war, with all of Dr. Holland's unsparing denunciations of secession and disloyalty, had intervened between the time when he brought order out of chaos in the Vicksburg schools, and the time in which his books had made their way to that notable strategic point, yet the *Sentinel* said: "Dr. Holland is remembered here as the principal of our Main Street public school, and as the scholarly preceptor of many of our boys who are now the leading citizens of this place. To his administration Vicksburg is largely indebted for the successful and honored history of this justly celebrated school."

The New York *Evening Post*, in a carefully prepared article, said: "No literary man in America perhaps, was so accurately fitted for his precise work. He had the immense advantage of keeping on a plane of thought just above that of a vast multitude of readers, each one of whom he could touch with his hand and raise a little upward. . . . He thought the thoughts of the average American citizen, he stated those thoughts with admirable good sense, and he fortified them with a moral standard uniformly high. Hence his popularity really travelled westward on the wave of our national civilization; to the more staid and critical East, it was a constant amazement to see the extent of his fame; but once beyond the Alleghanies his books sold by scores, and perhaps hundreds, where even Longfellow and Whittier sold by twos and threes. Certainly, if ever seer or prophet knew to whom he had been sent, it was Dr. Holland, and joyfully accepting it as from God, he wrought for them."

Said the *New York Tribune*: "He knew for whom he was writing, and he was more anxious to persuade than to startle them. . . . For young writers especially he had always a word of kindness and encouragement, and he never forgot, didactic as he was, that charity is better than censoriousness, and that criticism may be at once accurate and unjust. Nothing which he wrote could have made his readers worse—a great deal which he wrote ought to have made them better."

The New York *World* sums up an entertaining account of his home and surroundings thus: "While he holds his own opinions tenaciously, he is altogether tolerant of the opinions of others, and reckons among some of his best friends men and women of the art tribe who are radicals and rationalists in matters of belief."

The New York *Sun* began by calling him "*The Most Popular of Authors*," not only of this country but of England, and called attention to the fact that "he was one of the few authors of the United States who have made a fortune out of literature. It is true that he was besides successful as a newspaper and magazine proprietor, but his literary fame was the foundation of it all. As a rule, however great may be the reward a writer gets in reputation, in hard cash his recompense is comparatively small. Dr. Holland, however, was one of those fortunate writers to whom the reward comes at once, and in actual money. . . . His publishers printed for him, during twenty years, fifteen volumes. . . . The combined circulation of these works, which were not sold at the present cheap prices for fiction, but at the old and comparatively high prices obtained for bound and copyrighted books, was so great that he received from them a total royalty remarkable in the history of literature. . . .

"However much the critics might find fault with him, the average run of people, of New England especially, were not afraid to call him their favorite novelist, their favorite essayist, and their favorite poet. He drew for them the characters they were accustomed to in their daily lives. He placed his heroes and heroines amid circumstances which were easily comprehended by the class to whom he appealed. . . ."

Evidently *The Sun*, while correctly analyzing the secret of his power, did not appreciate how thoroughly Dr. Holland comprehended the new religious spirit of the time, which certainly thinks more of character, and less of creed, than any one to whom the name Puritan can be justly applied.

That his writings touched chords that could respond, in regions far beyond the New England that he so faithfully depicted, the following, from the London *Academy*, shows: "To read his novels is a perpetual inspiration, and to the young, with their imaginative vigor, nothing could be more healthful. . . . America has produced few working editors whose influence has been so paramount and far-reaching; and few have displayed so much talent—as a poet, lecturer, essayist, and as a pure and high-minded novelist, who could sketch with remarkable power all that is best and worst in American society."

In the *Canadian Monthly* we find: "Enough that he belonged to the order of true poets, or *seers*, whose eyes have been touched to see the glorious realities that lie beyond the world of sight and sense. He has not unfitly been styled the 'Apostle of the Commonplace,' because it was his *forte* to touch with the light of poetry the common ways of life, to show the beauty that to the seeing eye may lie about the humblest paths."

But, after all, it was the noble life that so nearly came up to his proclaimed ideals that commanded the supreme homage. Said the Atlanta (Ga.) *Christian Index:* "Above all, his honest directness of purpose, his hatred of sham, his vigorous championing of truth and wholesomeness in the work of authorship, and the high standard of morality in literature and society, which was set up by him in theory, and so conspicuously illustrated in his own manly practice, made him not only one of the most successful, but one of the most useful and beneficial writers and authors of our age."

In the same strain of valuing character, the *Hartford Courant* speaks : "An earnest, reverent purpose was aimed at and fulfilled in his entire literary career. All honor to him for his lifelong honor of that which is best and dearest in human life—human love."

The Philadelphia *Inquirer* said: "To his sterling worth and attractive character are due the unfailing loyalty he inspired in those who labored with him and for him, and a circle of admirers reaching round the world will miss him sorely and mourn him long."

And the *Critic*—which had the best of reasons for knowing—said: "Perhaps no man in this country has helped so many persons on their path of life by written or spoken words of kindness or wise advice."

The Rural Home, of Rochester, called attention to the purity of his writings: "As a pure and ennobling influence he entered American homes." But it was in the columns of the distinctively "religious journals" that Dr. Holland found the fullest appreciation. They felt that a rare example of all that they strive to exalt had ceased to be among living men. Said the *New York Observer:* "Addressing himself to the hearts of the people, he won his way to a popularity not exceeded by any American writer of poetry or prose. His labors brought him wealth and the comforts and luxuries that wealth brings, and which no man deserves more truly than he who by the sweat of his brain adds to the happiness and moral improvement of millions."

A writer in the *Examiner and Chronicle* who knew him well says: "In quietness he worked and ate his own bread. He studied to be quiet, and I can never think of him without a feeling of restful enjoyment. Dr. Holland was resolute, patient, judicious, and industrious. He was exceptionally endowed with tact and pluck and pertinacity. He was painstaking, and willing to bide his time. No rebuff could dishearten him. It was perfectly natural for him to go at it, and stick at it, to try again and keep trying. His first manuscripts were refused by some publishers, who would not look the way of him or them. There was one exception, Charles Scribner. He was an exceptional man, and he found in Holland's writings just what their readers by tens of thousands have found in them, wholesome counsel, salutary restraint, words of good cheer for the faint-hearted. Publisher and author had traits of character in common. Both were quiet, manly men, direct and upright in method, minding each his own business, and minding it shrewdly and assiduously. His fondness for his family was very beautiful. He said to me the other day at Bonnie-Castle, 'My children have had a long and sunny childhood, and that was just as I wished it.'

"He was fair in his estimates of his contemporaries. He spoke freely of their excellences, and seldom alluded to their defects. His indignation was stirred by meanness and chicanery, and then he was severe, but he had nothing but pitiful and hopeful words for the well-meaning who were overtaken in a fault or a blunder."

The editor of the New York *Evangelist*, himself a New England man, was a settled pastor in West Springfield at the time when the *Republican* began to make itself felt as a moral censor and power. He writes: "The chief criticism urged against Dr. Holland's productions was that they preached. Yes; but they preach the gospel of truth and a divine charity; they all expose and condemn what is vicious, however alluring its form may be. They all set forth a high ideal of life and character. His intellectual house had windows on all sides; but while enjoying the broad and diverse views in all directions, personally, he kept close to the hearthstone of the old faith, on which the fire ever burned. Doubtless much of his popular success was owing to the remarkable skill and novelty with which he presented old and obvious truths; but they were always truths of the greatest importance. The multiplication-table is commonplace and the golden rule a platitude, but commerce could not be carried on without the former, and the latter carries with it the promise of the millennium. In private life he exemplified what he commended in his writings. He was sincere, cordial, generous, sympathetic, considerate of others, tender as a woman, gentle as a child, brave as any knight in his loyalty to the right."

When accused of teaching heresy in his very early days in Springfield he read a chapter from the New Testament, saying, "That is my creed." In that early day he had a prescient perception of the new valuation that was coming to be put upon elaborate and metaphysical "systems of belief," spun from the brains of cloistered theologians, and in sharp contrast with the spirit of the Master, which is ever repeating, "This *do*."

The *Christian Union*, a live organ of a live religion, said : " Dr. Holland's literary appeal lay not to a range of facts and experiences which are the outgrowth of an advanced stage of mental or social culture ; he touched rather those central facts and experiences in which all classes find a common life. His work was moral rather than intellectual, and hence, although less brilliant, it was far more useful and permanent in its influence than much that has been done in the same lines more pretentiously. Intellectual ideals are for the few, moral ideals for the many ; and when Dr. Holland made himself the interpreter of the latter he became as the voice of their own souls to a host whom nature or circumstances had made mute. To be the apostle of the commonplace—if that were a true description of Dr. Holland—is to be the teacher of a great truth to great multitudes. Most lives are set in commonplace surroundings, are filled with commonplace incidents, are begun and ended in commonplace ways ; birth, marriage, work, suffering, and death are the universal commonplaces through which men pass from the cradle to the grave. The poet whose insight discovers some new and beautiful truth is a minister to the higher needs of men, and his service is generously recognized; but is he not equally the benefactor of his race who, walking along the common paths of life, turns the weeds into flowers and makes the dusty way bright with promise and radiant with hope? To idealize the commonplace is often more difficult than to disclose the poetic side of those inspiring truths which are a pillar of fire to the eyes of a few cultured souls, but for the multitude a vague and formless cloud. To interpret common events for common men is to enrich life where it is poorest, to brighten it where it is darkest, to make it inspiring where it is most depressing, to turn it into poetry where it is most prosaic.

"The upper ranges of truth and fact are always poetic to those who have spiritual insight; they are the mountain-peaks whose foreheads are always luminous, but blessed truly is he who brings the glow of aspiration and poetry into the valleys and makes apparent their common heritage of sunshine with the hills. Dr. Holland took the common experiences of life and made them deeply significant and beautiful to a multitude who would otherwise be only hewers of wood and drawers of water; he preached the gospel of a divine purpose in the wearisome details and the vexatious trials which are the staple of most men's lives. The dumb yearning of the boy on the farm for knowledge, the hard struggle of the young man for place and influence, the courage of vigor and maturity, the calmness and resignation of age, the lasting romance of love when marriage has made it the yoke-fellow with duty, the undying sweetness of family relationships, the blessed fruits of sorrow patiently borne, all these, which are the Bitter-sweet of human life, Dr. Holland has interpreted with a warm heart, a clear intelligence, and an undoubted poetic insight.

"And whatever excellence was in his literary work was also in his character and life. His career was harmonious, and in its way eminently successful, because the outer life expressed so fully and clearly the inner; because action followed so close upon thought; because kind words, helpful deeds, and single-hearted rectitude were the natural outcome of a loyal heart, an aspiring soul, and a true and genuine manhood."

This consensus of opinion has been quoted at such great length because it was the estimate of contemporary men who had watched Dr. Holland's development and career and influence from its beginning to its sudden close, and who naturally asked, but in the true spirit of philosophical inquiry, as to what was the secret of the marvellous adaptation of his work to the needs of such remarkable numbers of men, as unquestionably attested by the unprecedented total sale of his books and the great popularity of his magazine.

Was it not because he showed men and women their own best thoughts and judgments in words that they understood? When he told a youth of unscholarly make, but who could appreciate the dignity and seeming ease of a professional career, that it was a mistaken waste of power for such as he to go to college, in his own plain but convincing way, generally the youth saw the point. He was an eminently sane writer. The New England farmer called him a "sensible" writer, while if a page of Lowell or Emerson treating of the same questions had been read to him he would have said, "Perhaps he knows what he is talking about, I'm sure I don't." Though the works of these men teem with vigorous instruction, many of their expressions are like syncopations that require much classical learning, much knowledge of past history, and much philosophy in the mind of the reader, to be fully interpreted to him. Dr. Holland stated his thought, taking little of all these for granted, with a careful elaboration, under an unspoken, perhaps an unowned coercion, from the knowledge that his audience was busy men and women with little time for deep study and less for abstract speculation. On being questioned once as to the sources of literary power, he said: "I look into my heart and write," and many men found that he had expressed with masterly good sense just what they had been thinking and feeling. Thus he became their Voice. And then he had that high type of moral courage that dared to change an opinion when he saw good reasons for so doing; he fearlessly followed Holmes's advice, "Don't be consistent, but be simply true." He was willing to grow up into the full tree called for by the influences of his time, and the circumstances of his life, when planted in a broad space, drawing nourishment from many diverse sources, instead of remaining dwarfed in the pot in which the seedling had been temporarily planted, merely because it had been planted in it.

He was not always looking backward over his shoulder, but bravely, and at the risk of being misunderstood, followed Emerson's precept: "Speak what you think now in hard words, and to-morrow speak what to-morrow thinks in hard words again, though it contradict everything you said to-day."

Being convinced in his inmost soul that God wanted just such a man as he was in the time and place in which he had put him, he dared to be utterly true to his inmost self, and therefore this life lived in accordance with fixed principles, when viewed as a whole, presents a remarkably symmetrical picture, no matter from what angle it is looked at.

Will his writings always be popular? *Always* is a long time, and the men divinely appointed to supply the mental pabulum of their time, and who speak the potent word to it, appear duly in their epoch, being an inseparable and foreordained part of it, though the thoughts to which they give utterance may be as old as the Garden of Eden itself. If we look back and ask who reads the authors that were adored and canonized in the middle of—say the last century—we shall have to own that the reading is confined to a limited circle of persons justly called *literati*, and scholars with specialties to study up. In his own appointed time this Great Apostle to the Plain People did a great work: his thought and impulse is "built in" to the characters of a generation of noble men and women, who are still impressing their day with lofty views of *Duty*, at whose shrine he ever faithfully worshipped.

He left the beloved wife, who now resides in Orange, N. J.; two daughters—Annie, married to Mr. John Kasson Howe, now of Albany, N. Y.; Kate, the wife of Mr. Bleecker Van Wagenen (of Dodd, Mead & Co., New York)—and Mr. Theodore Holland, of Denver, Col., also married, all settled in the home-life that was so precious to their father.

The record on his monument shows his age to have been sixty-two years—not a long life as men ordinarily reckon longevity, but very long measured by the poet's standard:

"We should count time by heart-throbs. He most lives
Who thinks most, feels the noblest, acts the best."

HIS LAST RESTING-PLACE

When Mr. Samuel Bowles lay dying he said: "There is nothing the matter of me but thirty-five years of hard work," and if one cons the list of successful editors they are not a long-lived race, and as it is "not work but worry that kills," it is easy to believe that the pressure to have just so much done on time creates the necessity for a strenuous style of effort, under which the very springs of life must eventually snap. That last sentence from Dr. Holland's pen, lying as he left it on his desk for the "next issue," was a picture of the editorial life and its ceaseless demands.

He sleeps in the Springfield Cemetery—in sight of the Mount Holyoke that formed the background of all his early imaginings, and of which he has written, "it is a field laid out by God's own hand as a sleeping-place for his children. A tinkling brook dragged its silver chain over the pebbles through the midst of it, and old gnarled oaks with scanty foliage spread their arms and nodded upon its hillsides, and maples rose on every hand, so darkly and freshly green in summer, and so richly draped in gold and purple in autumn, that they betrayed the crystal springs which gushed at their roots, and laughed and played like children among the alders. The springs had been taught a new path to the valley, and there sprang like living trees, swaying and dissolving, sighing and whispering, in the midst of their crystal basins. . . . To this beautiful spot were borne the dead. It became the resting-place of the people—so beautiful that the living never tired of wandering through it, and lingering in it, and so sweet with its music of brooks and trees and fountains, and the sight and smell of flowers, that death became more amiable in the association."

His family have erected to his memory a monument of granite, which bears in one face a most accurate and life-like bronze medallion of him. The capital is surrounded by a wreath of the Bittersweet that he endowed with an imperishable vitality, and on one face are engraved those words from his will, which reveal the fountain whence he derived this strength and show the ideal that was as a pillar of fire by night to him :

"I am thankful for having enjoyed the privileges of labor and influence, thankful for wife and children, thankful for all my successes. I have intentionally and consciously wronged no man, and if I know my heart I have forgiven all my enemies. For the great hereafter I trust in the Infinite Love, as it is expressed to me in the life and death of my Lord and Saviour, Jesus Christ."

DR. HOLLAND'S GRAVE
At Springfield, Mass

www.ingramcontent.com/pod-product-compliance
Lightning Source LLC
Chambersburg PA
CBHW021817230426
43669CB00008B/779